AF589208

NO ORDINARY WOMEN

ALSO BY
P. O'CONNELL PEARSON

Fly Girls

Fighting for the Forest

Conspiracy

We Are Your Children Too

P. O'CONNELL PEARSON

NO ORDINARY WOMEN

How Progressive Era Reformers Reshaped America

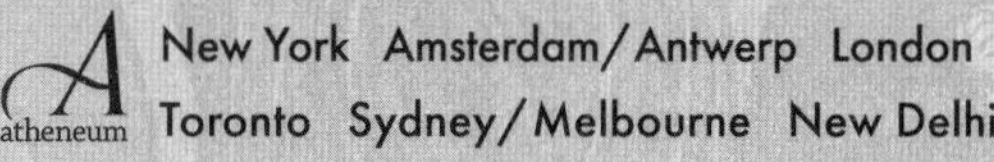
atheneum
New York Amsterdam/Antwerp London
Toronto Sydney/Melbourne New Delhi

ATHENEUM BOOKS FOR YOUNG READERS
An imprint of Simon & Schuster Children's Publishing Division
1230 Avenue of the Americas, New York, New York 10020

Jacket design by Greg Stadnyk

Interior design by Irene Metaxatos
The text for this book was set in Minion Pro.
Manufactured in the United States of America
0526 FFG
First Edition
2 4 6 8 10 9 7 5 3 1
Library of Congress Cataloging-in-Publication Data
Names: Pearson, P. O'Connell (Patricia O'Connell) author
Title: No ordinary women : how Progressive era reformers reshaped America / P. O'Connell Pearson.
Description: First edition. | New York : Atheneum Books for Young Readers, 2026. | Includes bibliographical references. | Audience: Ages 10 up | Audience: Grades 7–9 | Summary: "Acclaimed author P. O'Connell Pearson tells the inspiring story of the trailblazing women of the Progressive movement and their work that led to political, economic, and social change that impacts us to this very day"—Provided by publisher.
Identifiers: LCCN 2025026576 (print) | LCCN 2025026577 (ebook) | ISBN 9781665956222 hardcover | ISBN 9781665956246 ebook
Subjects: LCSH: Progressivism (United States politics)—History—Juvenile literature | Women social reformers—United States—Juvenile literature | Wealth—United States—Juvenile literature | CYAC: Progressivism (United States politics) | Women social reformers | Wealth | BISAC: JUVENILE NONFICTION / Girls & Women | JUVENILE NONFICTION / History / United States / 20th Century
Classification: LCC E743 .P417 2026 (print) | LCC E743 (ebook) | DDC 303.48/40973—dc23/eng/20251204
LC record available at https://lccn.loc.gov/2025026576
LC ebook record available at https://lccn.loc.gov/2025026577

For the thousands of women
and men who did the hard work
of reforming and reshaping
the United States during the
Progressive Era, and to those
who are fighting to preserve that
reform and protect American
democracy today

CONTENTS

NO ORDINARY WOMEN

CHAPTER 1

★★★

The Very Wealthy

On a cold January night in 1893, Mrs. Caroline Astor held a ball at her mansion on Fifth Avenue in New York City (on the exact spot where the Empire State Building stands today). She'd hosted the ball on the third Monday in January every year for more than two decades. Astor chose her guests from a list of the wealthiest people in New York. The Four Hundred, as they were known (though it wasn't clear exactly how many names were really on the list and Mrs. Astor didn't invite everyone at once, anyway), had more to offer than wealth alone. They were people who knew how to dress, what to say, and what not to say. They knew which of the gold-plated forks beside their gold-plated dishes to use first. They knew how to treat the servants, who wore velvety green coats with the made-up Astor coat of arms stamped on the buttons—the servants who brought out platter after platter of quail, partridge, truffles, terrapin, and more. In other words, these guests followed all the rules of New York Society. Who decided what those rules were? Mrs. Caroline Astor, of course.[1]

It took a lot of time and effort—as well as money—to earn a place on Mrs. Astor's list. And many of the Four Hundred admitted privately that the Astor parties were long and boring. So why did they all want an invitation? They wanted to see who else had been invited and to impress their fellow guests who saw them there. Perhaps strike a business deal. Maybe find a potential husband for their daughter. And so they arrived wearing very expensive suits or gowns, the women adorned in furs and feathers and jewelry. Lots of jewelry. But never as much jewelry as Mrs. Astor herself.

Caroline Astor was a plumpish woman who liked to stand very straight, chin held high, in front of an enormous portrait of herself as her glittering guests entered her home. She often wore a diamond tiara and a large diamond pin once owned by Marie Antoinette, the one-time queen of France. The queen who went to the guillotine during the French Revolution, partly because she'd been accused of spending France's wealth on herself. But Marie Antoinette's jewels weren't quite enough for Mrs. Astor. The leader of New York society added diamond and pearl bracelets and necklaces—some of them fake—to her outfit as well. One woman described her as "a walking chandelier."[2] A walking chandelier worth millions.

Caroline Astor's portrait, 1890

New York City was home

to half the nation's four thousand millionaires during the late 1800s (many of them would be billionaires in today's money). The rest were spread out in cities across the country. Some were quiet about their wealth. But many others did everything they could to be sure other people saw just how rich they were. One writer called that behavior "conspicuous consumption."[3] Mark Twain called the time period the "Gilded Age."

Imagine it. A millionaire in Baltimore had a gold-plated (gilded) bathtub and toilet.[4] The wife of another millionaire held a huge party for her dog. She bought the furry fellow a $15,000 (over $450,000 today) collar for the occasion.[5] A man in New York invited seventy people to dinner at the finest restaurant in the city. He paid $10,000 to have a lake built in the middle of the thirty-foot-long dining table. He then brought in live swans to glide gracefully back and forth in front of the guests. Unfortunately, the birds didn't understand what an elegant event the dinner was supposed to be—they spent most of the mealtime fighting with one another. Feathers flew as the diners tried to eat the sumptuous meal.

Other millionaires hosted costume balls where guests spent thousands on their outfits. Most of them dressed as kings and queens from every place and time, and wore actual jewels in their crowns. Many of these rich Americans were the descendants of people who had fought in the American Revolution. A bloody revolution to be rid of kings. Why would they now imitate royalty?

Parties were just one way to show off wealth. Houses were another. Mrs. Astor's ballroom and a table that could seat two hundred people were only the beginning. Many of the very rich in New York and other big cities built their own grand mansions. How grand? Some had over one hundred rooms. Masterpieces of art and sculpture (as well as expensive pieces with little artistic value) filled parlors and halls and ballrooms and galleries. At least seven individual members of the Vanderbilt family—one of the richest families in the world at the time—owned mansions along Fifth Avenue in New York. George W. Vanderbilt built a home in Asheville, North Carolina, that required over a thousand workers and six years to complete. The house had thirty-five bedrooms, forty-three bathrooms, and sixty-five fireplaces. Think of the trees those fireplaces consumed.[6] Vanderbilt hired more men to work in agriculture and forestry on his 125,000-acre estate than the US Department of Agriculture hired throughout the entire country at that time.[7]

Of course, one mansion wasn't enough for a lot of millionaires. They built seaside summer homes and sailed to them on their private yachts. Others traveled in privately owned railway cars to these summer "cottages." Cottages far bigger than the

Mrs. Astor's gallery-ballroom, 1897

White House. Multimillion-dollar cottages that sat empty most of the year.

How much money did these upper-crust Gilded Age people have? The millionaires and almost-millionaires who made up the richest 1 percent of Americans in 1890 owned over 50 percent of the nation's wealth.[8] Where did all that money come from?

"Summer cottage," Newport, Rhode Island, built in 1897 by Caroline Astor's daughter

Some of the rich, including the Astors and Vanderbilts, inherited their money from parents and grandparents who had made fortunes when the United States was a very young nation. Those ancestors had started businesses and done very well. Unfortunately, many of them—including John Jacob Astor Sr., the first Astor to arrive in the United States—used questionable business practices. Astor, for example, made his money in the fur trade on the West Coast in the early 1800s. He paid Indigenous

J. P. Morgan, 1902

people very little for the furs they brought to him. He then turned around and sold those furs at enormous prices in Eastern cities like New York and Boston. He also charged very high prices for the goods he sold in his trading posts, knowing that there was no other place to buy necessities. Many people called those business practices ruthless. Astor and other successful businessmen called their tactics smart business.

Many of the children and grandchildren of these men—such as Caroline Astor's husband, William—were happy to inherit the family wealth. But they never worked themselves. They just spent their "old money." Others worked hard and used their inheritance to make more money. J. P. Morgan followed his father and grandfather into the banking business. He increased his wealth, and then financed and organized railroad companies. Morgan also made deals to create the US Steel Corporation, General Electric, and International Harvester. His J. P. Morgan & Co. dominated the banking industry. He even loaned money to the United States government during at least two economic crises. By the 1890s, J. P. Morgan was considered the most important business leader in America.[9]

Caroline Astor considered families with "old money" worthy of her Four Hundred. But far more American millionaires in the late 1800s had "new money." Their money came from industries and businesses such as oil and electricity that hadn't existed a few years earlier. Caroline Astor didn't approve of that new money. She didn't like change or the men who were making fortunes from it. But the United States was evolving with astonishing speed in the late 1800s, whether Caroline Astor liked it or not.

Picture what had happened in just a few years.

When Astor, Morgan, and other old-money Americans were children, well over half of white Americans—about nine million people—lived on farms in the nation's twenty-six states. This was during the 1830s and 1840s. At that time, some three million Black Americans were enslaved and doing agricultural labor in the South. Most Indigenous peoples east of the Mississippi River had lost their tribal lands to white settlement. They'd been forced to move onto reservations or migrate to Canada. But many Native Americans west of the Mississippi River still lived in their traditional ways.

Farm tools and transportation hadn't changed very much in hundreds of years. A farmer's son learned to plow, plant, harvest, and drive a horse-drawn wagon just as his father and grandfather and great-grandfather had. "Women's work" hadn't changed much either. A girl learned skills from her mother—sewing by hand, baking bread, churning butter, raising vegetables, and so on. About half of free American children (but not enslaved children) had some formal education. More in the North. Fewer in the South. They often got through elementary school before quitting to take on full-time farmwork. Very few boys or girls went to high school, even in places that had high schools. Far fewer went to college.

By the late 1880s, slavery had been abolished and most Native Americans across the country had been forced onto reservations. A majority of Americans still lived in rural areas or small towns. But thousands of young people now left their family's farms and moved to cities. They wanted new jobs in new industries. Immigrants from southern and eastern Europe flooded into American cities for jobs too. In the far West—California, Oregon, and the Washington Territory—Chinese workers arrived. These immigrants faced the same kind of hostility that earlier groups of immigrants, particularly the Irish, had faced in the 1840s and '50s.

Blast furnaces, around 1900, at Carnegie's Homestead Steel Plant in Pennsylvania

The new city folk took jobs in clothing factories, meatpacking or food-canning plants, machine works, glassworks, and more. Others went to huge mining operations in mountain regions and dug miles of underground tunnels and shafts to find coal, iron ore, silver, gold, and copper. Still others found employment in mills producing new kinds of steel. Some worked laying railroad tracks as fast as those steel mills could produce them. Members of the Iroquois or Haudenosaunee nations came to cities too. In New

York City in particular, they became ironworkers on high bridges and skyscrapers.

Farmers also did their work differently by the 1880s. They could now join with neighboring farmers to share the cost of enormous steam-powered machines that plowed land and harvested many crops. They could move their crops to faraway markets by train rather than small, slow wagons. Homemakers could buy bread and butter and canned goods at a store instead of making them at home. They could use a sewing machine or even buy ready-made clothing from a department store or catalog. And travelers could cross the entire country by train in four or five days instead of four or five months in a wagon.

The transformation was astonishing. And frightening, at least for some people. Many felt like the earth was shifting under their feet. Others, including the men who became business "tycoons" or "magnates" and made all that new money, embraced the changes. These entrepreneurs took advantage of opportunities in the new economy and made bigger fortunes than even the Astors or Vanderbilts had.

John Davison Rockefeller, 1901

John D. Rockefeller—one of the richest men in American history—did not inherit any money. His father was often absent from home, moved the family frequently, and abandoned them in Cleveland, Ohio, when John was a teenager. As the oldest boy in a family of six children, John had to start earning money at a very young age. But Rockefeller managed to finish high school and find a job as a bookkeeper. He was smart, hardworking,

Andrew Carnegie, 1906

and serious, and he moved up the ranks quickly. In his early twenties, Rockefeller and a friend ran a business selling supplies to the US Army during the Civil War. From there, Rockefeller went into the new oil industry (oil had been discovered in Pennsylvania in 1859). Just over ten years later, John D. Rockefeller controlled most of the oil-refining industry in the United States. By 1900, he was worth almost a billion dollars (well over $300 billion in today's money).

Andrew Carnegie came to the United States from Scotland at the age of twelve and went to work sweeping floors in a cotton mill. He moved to better and better jobs as his employers saw his talent and ambition and gave him greater opportunities. He made the most of them. Twenty years later, Carnegie dominated steel production and was one of the wealthiest people in the world.

John D. Rockefeller, Andrew Carnegie, and other industrialists believed that they had earned every bit of their wealth on their own. After all, they'd created new ways of organizing and conducting business. They'd experimented with the best ways to produce new and better materials and goods. They'd found ways to cut costs. They'd invested in new ideas and took business and financial risks. In a short time, they had established the biggest companies the world had ever seen.

Critics could argue that most industrialists also used harsh business practices to buy up or ruin their competitors. They fired anyone who tried to organize workers or demand better conditions. And they happily benefited from the flood of immigrants pouring into the country. Men like Andrew Carnegie could pay their workers extremely low wages because those workers knew that thousands of newcomers were ready to take their jobs if they quit or demanded a higher wage.

However they achieved their success, the tycoons had transformed the United States from a nation of farmers into a powerhouse of industry. They made no apologies for any of their actions. It was just smart business, they said. And they believed they had earned their place as the leaders of industrial empires.

Many Americans looked up to these successful industrialists. They saw them as models of "rugged individualism"—the idea that people are entirely responsible for their own success or failure, no matter their circumstances.

The majority of American people had long believed in individualism. Not everyone could become a millionaire, of course. But men (hardly anyone considered women business-minded in those days) with the right attitude, gumption, and willingness to work hard could do very well. Even perfectly ordinary Americans might travel West and claim good farmland (never fair to the Indigenous people who already lived there, but most white Americans didn't think much about that). Or they might learn a skilled trade or open a small business. America was the land of opportunity. Wasn't it? Everyone could be richer than their ancestors were, right? The tycoons certainly thought so. John D. Rockefeller wrote:

> The failures which a man makes in his life are due almost always to some defect in his personality, some weakness of body, or mind, or character, will, or temperament.[10]

In other words, according to Rockefeller, poverty was usually a person's own fault.

As the twentieth century neared, millionaire American industrialists saw a bright future for their country. A future filled with more and more industry, success, and wealth. But they argued that such a future depended on continuing existing government policies—policies that had allowed their businesses to grow in the first place.

They were talking about the concept of "laissez-faire"—French for "let you do" or "leave alone." Laissez-faire is a policy of keeping the government out of business affairs. In a laissez-faire economy, the government does not tell businesses what products to make or how to make them. It doesn't tell businessmen how much to charge for their products. The government does not make rules or safety regulations for factories or mines. It doesn't tell employers how much to pay workers or how many hours anyone should work. Supporters of laissez-faire practices argue that the government should not be involved in how a business is run. If left alone, they say, business and manufacturing will naturally bring prosperity to the whole country, to everyone.

But while the tycoons said that they believed in laissez-faire policies, they used their profits to buy power and influence in government. They demanded and received free public land for railroads. They drilled oil wells and mined on government-controlled public lands without paying fees. They told members of Congress what laws to write, including tax laws that helped tycoons make more money. Congress obeyed. Members wouldn't be reelected if they didn't go along. The tycoons would use their wealth and influence to make sure of it.

Was that laissez-faire? Was the government really leaving businesses alone?

✣✣✣

By 1890, no one had more influence on America than business leaders like Morgan, Rockefeller, and Carnegie. Not even the United States government. Those businessmen saw themselves as "captains of industry." Their attitudes toward work, change, and upper-class society were different from those of the Astors and most other "old money" people. But these industrialists agreed with the Four Hundred that having millions of dollars felt very good. They also agreed with Mrs. Astor and the rest that the conditions, rules, and laws that had made them wealthy and powerful should stay just as they were. They knew what was best for the economy. They knew what was best for the country. There was no need to change the system.

Not everyone thought the way they did.

CHAPTER 2

★★★

The Working Poor

Many of Mrs. Caroline Astor's Four Hundred lived in New York City's Midtown and Upper East Side neighborhoods. So did many of the new-money millionaires. If any of them had strolled south along Fifth Avenue and Broadway, they would have entered a neighborhood known as the Lower East Side. Compared to their neighborhoods, it was another world. In reality, it was home to many of their parlor maids, ladies' maids, chamber maids, cooks, laundry workers, coachmen, footmen, and grooms. But most of the very rich either didn't want to know that or didn't care.

Immigrants had populated much of Manhattan's Lower East Side for a long time. *Lots* of immigrants—first Irish and German, then Italian and eastern European Jews. How many immigrants? The Lower East Side was the most densely populated, crowded place on earth in 1893. On average, more than eight hundred people lived in every acre of the neighborhood.[1] Picture a football field with eight hundred people living and working and shopping and moving around on it. Over 230,000 people within one square mile (in 2020, there were about 135 people per acre, or 88,000 people per square mile living in the Lower East Side).[2]

New York City children play in gutter near a dead horse, around 1900

On any morning, in any weather, men selling vegetables from carts called out in Russian. Other men and women with wagons of fruit, baked goods, or crafts shouted in German or Yiddish, some in Polish, in Italian, and some in English. Small children played between produce stalls and horse carts. Policemen with Irish accents walked the beat. Pedestrians stepped around garbage bins spilling over with stinking meat and rotting vegetables. The poorest residents kept an eye out for edible scraps in those bins. And everyone dodged piles of manure.

Imagine the scene. New York City had no effective sanitation system or street cleaning until about 1895. This was before

automobiles existed, and well over one hundred thousand horses moved through the city daily. They pulled wagons, carts, carriages, fire engines, and more. Each of those horses left some twenty to thirty pounds of manure on the streets every day. Do the math. That's *two to three million pounds* of manure in the streets *every day* (some sources estimate five million pounds of manure per day).

People like Mrs. Astor paid workers to clean the streets in front of their mansions and take away the garbage. Residents of the Lower East Side couldn't afford to do that. So the mud and manure and garbage sat there, attracting flies and rats and germs.

Most of the people in the Lower East Side lived in tenement apartment buildings that lined the streets. The buildings were four or five stories high with no elevators. The thirty or more people living in the four small apartments on each floor all shared one toilet built into a closet in the hallway. Many

Hester Street, the Lower East Side, 1902

buildings didn't even have that. Residents from all the apartments in a whole building often shared two or three outhouses in the tiny backyard. That was where the only water spigot was too. Residents had to take a bucket down to the yard and haul it back upstairs again every time they needed water.

Think about how easily disease spread in those conditions—no matter how hard anyone tried to keep their homes and families clean. Worse, apartments at the back of the building faced the outhouses and alleys where garbage attracted rats. It's estimated that one in five babies in those rear tenements died before reaching their first birthday.[3] Tuberculosis, a lung disease, and cholera, an intestinal disease, spread everywhere.

The tenement apartments had no heat other than a coal stove (air-conditioning didn't exist at the time), and light and air came from just two windows at one end of each apartment. Some buildings had no windows at all, and the only air came through a center shaft. Those shafts were terrible fire hazards, but it was an inexpensive way to build, and there were no fire codes for tenement owners to worry about.

Immigrant families pouring into New York from overcrowded ships accepted the jam-packed conditions because they had no choice. They needed to live within walking distance of their jobs in nearby factories or at the docks. Cars and buses hadn't been invented yet, and even the fare of a few pennies for the trolley was too much for most factory workers. Besides, many immigrants wanted to be near people who spoke their language and shared their culture.

Complaints about the buildings didn't help as more people in need of a place to live got off the ships or moved to the city from rural areas. If one person didn't like their tenement, ten more were waiting to take their place. And the very low wages factory owners and industrialists paid meant that most families couldn't afford anything better even if it did exist.

Who owned these buildings? Sometimes a resident was able to save money and invest in a tenement building. But many more tenements had millionaire owners who never saw the building or the neighborhood or its residents. Caroline Astor's husband, William B. Astor, owned a large number of tenements in New York City. Those tenements brought the Astors a lot of money when their managers collected rent from poor families every month. Many of the Astors' wealthy friends owned tenements too. Why didn't they make the apartments safer or more comfortable or charge less rent? Their goal was profit. And there were no laws or regulations telling owners like Mr. Astor and the others what they could or couldn't do. So they chose to make as much money with as little cost as possible.

✣✣✣

Immigrants on an Atlantic liner, around 1906

Rose Schneiderman was typical of the immigrants who lived in the Lower East Side. She'd arrived in New York City at the age of eight. Born in Poland (part of the Russian Empire at the time), Rose had gone to Hebrew school and attended a Russian elementary school before her parents decided to emigrate to the United States. Jewish people in the Russian Empire faced terrible prejudice and discrimination (anti-Semitism). The Schneidermans wanted a better life. They wanted a level of education and opportunity for their children that didn't exist in their home country.

Sadly, Rose's father died just two years after they settled in New York—right around the time Mrs. Astor was preparing for her 1893 ball. The family quickly fell into poverty, even though

New York City tenement yard, 1900

Mrs. Schneiderman worked as a skilled seamstress. No matter how many hours she worked, she couldn't support her four young children. Finally, she made the difficult decision to put the children in a Jewish orphanage rather than see them go hungry. She hoped it would be a temporary solution to her problems. But imagine how that must have felt to Rose and the younger children. How could their mother leave them with strangers? Would she come back?

Rose did her best to care for her siblings at the orphanage. When they reunited with their mother sometime later, she continued to look after them while Mrs. Schneiderman worked all hours. Even so, money was still a problem and Rose had to quit school as soon as she finished the sixth grade at thirteen. She found a job in a department store and began work. A few years later, she moved to a job in a cap factory, part of the garment industry—New York City's biggest business.

Factories and "sweatshops" in New York produced over 50 percent of all the ready-made clothing sold in the United States.[4] In tenement sweatshops, men, women, and sometimes children—some as young as five or six—worked all day at sewing jobs in the same small apartments where they lived. They crowded around a table or sat on beds or stools, straining their eyes in the dim light. Employers gave the homeworkers fabric, told them what to make, and paid the workers for each piece of clothing they completed. But even with five or six people working ten or more hours a day, there was never enough money. So people worked late into the night if they could find light. They worked when they were ill. And many families had to rely on their children to help with the sewing or take care of younger siblings instead of going to school or playing or anything else. The money still wasn't enough.

Miss Rose Schneiderman, between 1909 and 1920

Factory work like the kind Rose Schneiderman did for a bigger garment business probably meant brighter light and a more efficient work surface. But the hours and pay weren't much better than a home factory. And bigger businesses usually had strict rules against talking, taking breaks, and the like. Those garment factories in New York hired thousands upon thousands of workers. Keeping wages low for everyone—and especially low for women and children—meant bigger profits for business owners. The owners could offer such low wages because if someone

Garment workers, 1913

Jewish family working on garters in kitchen

didn't want the job, a thousand more people were eager for any kind of work.

Other cities had their own dominant industries. In Chicago, slaughterhouses and meatpacking plants hired more workers than any other business. Magnates like Gustavus Swift and Philip Armour made fortunes with those trades. But the stockyards, slaughterhouses, and plants were dangerous, unhealthy places to work. Places where men and boys lost fingers, or hands, or their lives. In Atlanta, it was cotton mills

Cotton mill, Texas, 1913

and iron foundries, though agriculture dominated most of the South. In Evansville, Indiana, the largest factories and plants made farming equipment and wagons. And Pittsburgh's biggest industry was steel.

At the Carnegie Steel Company, men worked twelve hours a day, seven days a week, with *one* day off each year—the Fourth of July. Overheated men drank whole buckets of water as they shoveled coal into giant blast furnaces. They wore wooden shoes because the heat was so intense that it melted leather. They wrapped their faces and necks in water-soaked scarves. Even so, the heat seared their lungs and blackened and blistered their skin. In return for eighty hours of dangerous labor a week, they made about ten dollars, a bit more than other mills paid.[5] It was enough to buy basic food for a family, but not nearly enough to also pay for a decent place to live. Even so, Carnegie instructed the men who ran the company for him to be always on the lookout for ways to cut costs, including wages. That was the case in most industries.

Outside the cities, men and boys traveled as much as a mile underground into mines every day. They worked there for twelve hours, digging for coal, silver, gold, or other metals by lantern light. Picture that. Those miners saw daylight only on Sundays. The rest of their lives were spent in the dark.

Breathing in coal dust or other toxins often led to lung disease and early death. The miners' widows and young children then faced eviction from the houses they rented from the mining companies. The same thing happened in steel mill towns and any place where the business owned its workers' housing.

Steel and iron mills, Sharon, Pennsylvania, 1905

Railroad workers, mostly Chinese and Irish immigrants, faced terrible living conditions. They worked in baking heat and bitter cold, often using deadly explosives with almost no protection as they tunneled through mountains. For all that, they experienced constant racial and religious prejudice and discrimination in addition to very low wages.

Miners 2.5 miles underground, Illinois

In all these industries, a worker who was injured on the job was out of luck. And a lot of workers ended up injured, since there were no laws or regulations requiring safety precautions or equipment. There was no insurance or help of any kind for someone who couldn't work, either. Even if a faulty machine had caused the injury. Bosses simply hired another expendable worker. Like landlords, business tycoons could do as they pleased.

Where could industrial workers find an opportunity to do well in such circumstances? Could these people—from a child

End of track, Humboldt Plains, Nevada

garment worker to a hardened miner—become well-off if only they worked harder? Was it even possible to work any harder than these people did?

Tycoons answered that any worker was free to quit their job and go elsewhere if the situation was so terrible. They could do what earlier Americans had done—go West, or learn a trade and get a better industrial job, or open a small business. But there were several problems with that argument.

Yes, skilled workers sometimes managed to save money and move to better jobs and better housing. Children who could stay in school could advance further when they did start to work. Some immigrants arrived with enough money to start their own businesses and were successful. Their stories encouraged more immigration and gave newcomers hope. For most workers, though, those stories were just dreams. Why?

By the end of the nineteenth century, there was almost no unclaimed land in the West. Once the government had pushed Indigenous people onto reservations, white settlers had flooded into the newly open land. There was no more frontier, no real wilderness waiting to be settled by ambitious newcomers.

Most factory, mill, and mining jobs offered almost no way to move up within the business. And while Carnegie's employers had helped him along the way because they saw how smart he was and how hard he worked, workers in the new economy (including Carnegie's steel mills) never even met the men who employed them. Industrialists didn't notice their workers at all. At the same time, small businesses struggled to compete with the huge corporations that gobbled them up in every industry.

As a result of these changes and the attitudes of tycoons, at least 40 percent of workers in American factories, mills, and stores lived in poverty.[6] And more workers were injured or killed in accidents on the job in the United States than almost anywhere else in the world during the late 1800s.[7] Workers didn't know those statistics, of course. But they did know that they were fed up. Many began to question the belief that hard work and good character would bring a person prosperity in the United States. They weren't alone. Americans who belonged to the new "middle class" were asking the same questions.

Then, Now, and In-Between: The Wealth Gap

The "wealth gap" is the difference in economic worth between one group and another.

Then: During the late 1800s, the richest 1 percent of American families owned more than 50 percent of the nation's wealth. It may have been much more, but no one was collecting data at the time. Either way, we can say for certain that the gap between the richest Americans and everyone else was enormous.

Now: Today, governments, credit companies, and banking businesses around the world collect detailed financial information. In 2024, those sources showed that the top 10 percent of households in the US had over 67 percent of the nation's wealth. The bottom 50 percent of the population shared 2.5 percent of that wealth.[8] And three individuals in the US controlled more wealth than the bottom 50 percent of the country put together.[9]

These particular numbers then and now don't say anything about the individuals who have or don't have wealth. They don't tell us if a person at the top is generous with her wealth or a miser. They don't say if a successful business owner pays his employees well or not. The numbers don't tell us if someone near the bottom is lazy or in poor health or chooses to live simply. They also don't tell us what the effects of a huge wealth gap are. That's something that economists and politicians argued about more than a hundred years ago. They still argue about it today.

What the numbers do tell us is that the wealth gap of

the late 1800s and the wealth gap of today are similar. In both time periods, the difference between the few people at the very top and the millions in the bottom half is gigantic.

In-Between: Has a wealth gap like this always existed? In short, no.

During the late 1800s and early 1900s, the very wealthy constantly controlled at least 40 percent of all the wealth in the United States. But starting in about 1940, the percentage of wealth held by the top 1 percent decreased and continued to decrease for the next thirty years. The top 1 percent didn't lose any actual money. But people at the lower end of the wealth scale began to do better. How can that be?

We often think of the nation's total wealth as a pie. If the pie is always the same size and one group of people increases their share, then another group's share has to decrease. But the economic pie *isn't* always the same size. During the middle of the twentieth century, the nation's wealth increased. The pie got bigger. That meant that 99 percent of the country could have a bigger share without taking any actual money from the people at the top.

In 1970, the top 1 percent of the country had more money than they did in 1940. But that wealth was only about 25 percent of the total. The wealth of middle-class and lower-class Americans had risen as the pie got bigger. How? Regulations and laws increasing the minimum wage (the lowest amount an employer is allowed to pay his employees) helped workers. So did labor unions that bargained for better wages and

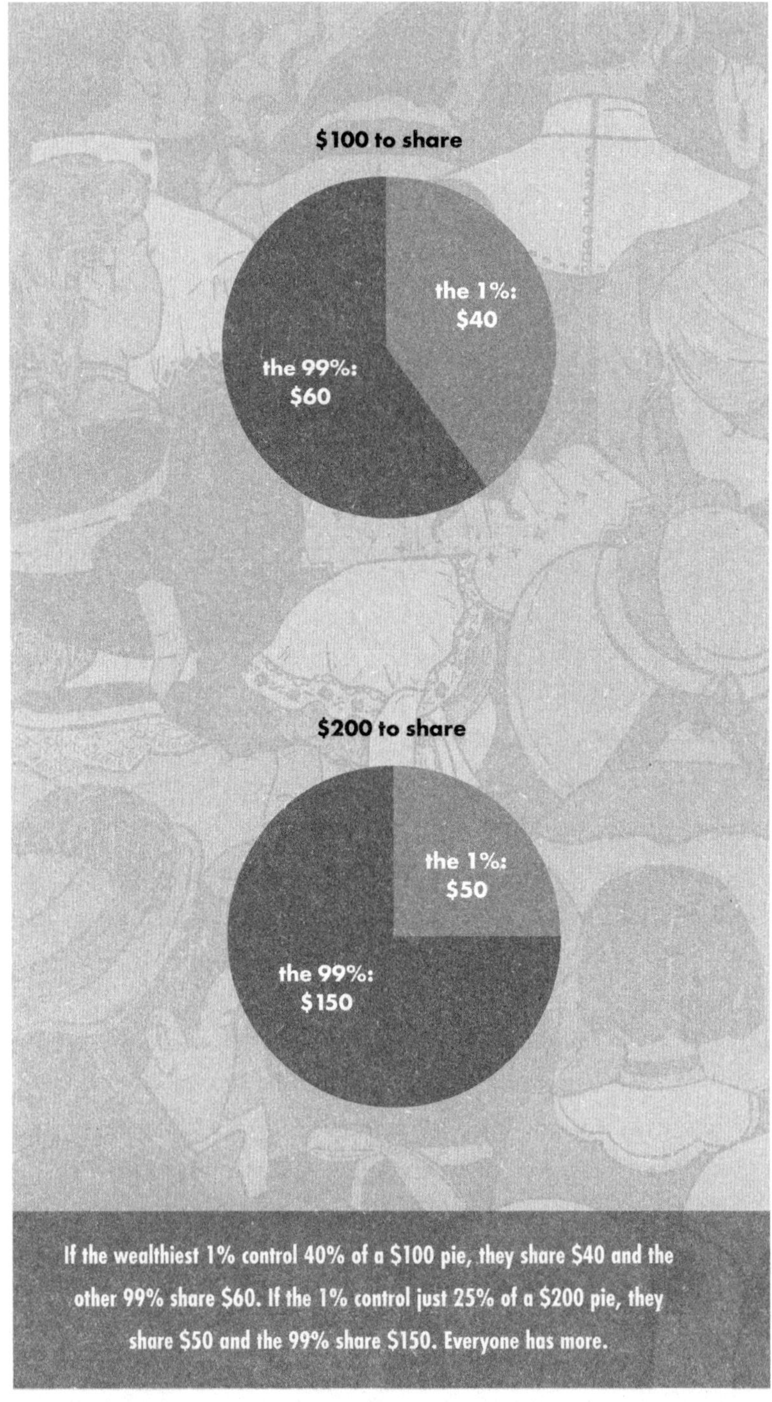

If the wealthiest 1% control 40% of a $100 pie, they share $40 and the other 99% share $60. If the 1% control just 25% of a $200 pie, they share $50 and the 99% share $150. Everyone has more.

benefits. And the average American worker had more education than ever before. This increased production and innovation, and pushed wages even higher.

Then, in the late 1970s, a shift began. Congress had lowered the percentage a person had to pay in income taxes (the tax rate) during the 1960s. When Ronald Reagan became president in 1981, he asked Congress to lower income tax rates and business taxes even more. The new tax laws benefited wealthy people much more than any other group. A person with a small income might pay a few hundred dollars less per year in taxes, while a wealthy person might pay hundreds of thousands of dollars less. The same thing happened with businesses.

The idea was that lower taxes and fewer business regulations would encourage wealthy business owners and businesses to expand, create more jobs, and improve their industries. That should benefit everyone from the very top to the lowest worker. The arguments in favor of these economic policies were very similar to the arguments made by the tycoons of the late 1800s.

The economy did improve in some ways during the Reagan years. The wealthiest Americans—especially people in the banking and financial industry—gained wealth, and the economic pie grew. But businesses did *not* invest in their workers. In fact, workers' wages did not even keep up with rising costs. A worker's situation does not improve if her salary goes up $100 per month and her rent goes up $150.

During those same years, corporations changed the way they paid their top leaders, their CEOs. Back in the 1960s and 1970s, the heads of big corporations such as

Ford and General Electric made about twenty to thirty times more than their company's workers did. That's a big difference, but nothing like the days when Carnegie made four thousand times what his workers did.[10] In the 1990s, though, CEOs and other business leaders' incomes began to rise rapidly.

And so: By 2020, CEOs made almost four hundred times more than their workers. While average worker wages increased about 18 percent between 1980 and 2020, CEO compensation increased more than 1,000 percent.[11] And with costs for goods and shelter rising more than 18 percent, workers could afford less and less.

The wealth gap today is close to what it was over one hundred years ago.

CHAPTER 3

★★★

From the Middle

As a child in the 1870s, Lillian Wald had never thought much about millionaires or the poor. She'd never met anyone like Caroline Astor or Andrew Carnegie while she was growing up. She'd never met anyone like Rose Schneiderman, either. The Wald family was part of the group known today as the "middle class"—people who weren't wealthy, but who were much better off than those working in mills, mines, and factories. Lillian's parents were not millionaires or even almost-millionaires. They didn't have mansions or yachts or swans on the dining room table. But they lived very comfortably.

Lillian's father sold optical goods (glass lenses) in Rochester, New York. Her mother, Minnie, was a homemaker. Max Wald did well in his work, and Minnie Wald felt fulfilled and happy in her role as wife and mother. She was grateful that she could devote herself to motherhood and homemaking.

As a child, Lillian and her three siblings had no way of knowing how fortunate they were. Wald later described herself as a "spoiled" child. She was surrounded by nearby uncles, aunts, and grandparents, and lived in a house that seemed to be always filled with family and music and laughter. She went to a private school, and had more than enough food, beautiful clothing, books, and toys. Her grandfather even gave each of the four Wald children a pony—every one of them named Kitty.[1]

Yet Lillian wasn't really *spoiled* in the way that word is often used today. Yes, she had comforts that most children did not have. But her parents made sure that she and her brothers and sister did not grow up selfish or demanding or irresponsible. The Wald children were expected to do well in school and they did. They were expected to show good manners and they did. They also learned the importance of caring for others as they watched their parents and other family members giving time, talent, and money to a variety of charities, often through their synagogue.

There were more middle-class Americans like the Walds in the late 1800s than there had ever been before. Years earlier, most people in the United States worked on farms. Farmers could generally take care of their families. But they couldn't buy extras the way the country's tiny middle class could. That middle class consisted of some well-off farmers and planters, as well as doctors, lawyers, craftsmen, successful shop owners, and so on. They made enough money to have comfortable houses and a few luxuries. They could afford to educate their sons (few girls went beyond elementary school at the time) and build savings. They made up about 5 percent of the population.

That changed with the new industries that brought huge wealth to the tycoons of the late 1800s. Men like Carnegie and Rockefeller couldn't run their enormous companies alone. Think about it. They needed lawyers to write contracts, clerks to keep records, accountants to track the money, managers to oversee workers, engineers to design new equipment—on and on. Those "white-collar" jobs—called that because men who worked in offices usually wore white shirts with their suits and ties—required education. A man with an education could demand good pay. He could afford a nice house on a quiet street, away from the docks or smokestacks or noise and dirt of factories and mills. He might be able to send his sons to college, buy a good carriage and a piano, and hire a maid or cook to help at home.

By 1890, about 20 percent of Americans were in the middle class (today, the middle class is about 50 percent of the population).[2] Some, like the Wald family, were quite well off. Others were closer to the working class—miners, factory workers, maids, cooks, and the like. But lower middle-class people were still confident that they could feed and clothe their children and keep them in school.

Telephone operator at work, 1922

The new technologies that opened up opportunities for middle-class men also offered young women socially respectable job options for the first time. Women with some education could work as telephone operators or typists, or in other office positions. Those jobs didn't pay much. And most young women worked only a short time before quitting to marry and take up their careers as homemakers. Even so, many parents didn't approve of their daughters' brief independence. They believed that young ladies should not do any kind of paid work. It was considered "unwomanly."

Minnie Wald agreed. Like most middle-class Americans at

Woman at typewriter, 1892

the time, she believed that a woman's place was in the home. She wanted her daughters to find the kind of happiness and fulfillment she enjoyed in the domestic sphere.

Middle-class and upper-class Americans of the 1800s generally accepted the idea that men and women were meant to have different roles in society. Men worked to support a family financially. They dealt in business affairs and political matters. Women were thought to be too "virtuous" for that. A woman's role or sphere was "domestic"—at home. It was up to her to make a warm and loving environment, a safe and serene place away from the chaos of the outside world. It was a woman's job to raise healthy and moral children. These divisions between men and women, people in many parts of the world believed, were part of God's and nature's plan. Of course, only those with some wealth could afford to think this way. Poor women had always worked to make money, often in the homes of middle-class and upper-class women.

Minnie Wald was pleased when Lillian's older sister, Julia, married young and set up housekeeping. Julia looked forward to becoming a mother and seemed content in the domestic sphere. Lillian was another story.

Wald wasn't exactly rebellious. She did all the things a middle-class young lady was supposed to do. She did well in school, studied music, went to dances and socials, and dressed very fashionably. She was good at most things she tried, though she was easily bored with teas and socials. And she admitted to being terrible at embroidery. But embroidery didn't matter to Lillian. Neither did most other domestic skills. Lillian Wald simply couldn't picture herself going straight from school and her childhood home to marriage, motherhood, homemaking, and more teas and socials.

Wald hoped to go to college. This was another new option for women whose families could afford it. Only a small handful of US colleges had admitted women before the Civil War. But during the two decades after the war, several state universities opened their doors to women, and a number of women's colleges were founded. Lillian didn't know what she would study, or what she would do after college. But she felt a need for "serious, definite work."[3] Important work. Not that keeping a house and raising a family wasn't serious—it was serious, important, and challenging work. It just wasn't for her. Not yet, anyway.

Lillian finished high school with excellent marks at a time when fewer than 5 percent of young people completed high school at all.[4] Sadly, though, her college dreams evaporated when tragedy struck the family. A drowning accident took the life of her older brother, Alfred. Lillian was devastated. Her mother was completely shattered. Minnie Wald suddenly seemed fragile, broken. With Julia married and out of the house, Lillian hesitated to leave home. She decided to stay with her parents, at least for a while. She didn't want to be idle, so she took an office job at an uncle's financial company. There was nothing wrong with the work, but it didn't feel important to Lillian. She was soon restless and wishing for . . . for what? She didn't know.

Lillian Wald wasn't the only middle-class young woman looking for something more than a life in the traditional domestic sphere. Thousands of young women all over the country felt the same way. The few who had college degrees wanted professional work, but most careers were closed to women. Others who had finished high school or a little bit of college looked for ways to make use of their education and the skills they had developed. And some who'd entered the domestic sphere of marriage and children wanted to participate in a world beyond their own homes. Many of these young women wanted to help solve the problems that worried middle-class Americans.

Why would people like the Walds be worried? They had very

good lives. But they also had access to more information and news than anyone, anywhere, at any time had ever had. And that news had a lot of people on edge.

The middle class got news from all over the country through newspapers and magazines (radio and television hadn't yet been invented). More and more publications had started up as new technologies reduced the cost of printing and new railroad lines offered quick, inexpensive mail delivery.

Local and widespread publications printed ads for new products—from ready-made clothing to carpet sweepers to fountain pens and zippers. Local papers also reported on events from births, deaths, and marriages to the winner of the county fair's baking contest. Bigger publications reported on bigger stories—discoveries and inventions, crimes and disasters, politics and economics.

Some nationally known papers and magazines also began printing articles based on "investigative reporting." Investigative journalists dug deep into a story. They looked at things the way a detective might. Americans could now sit in their parlors and read about corruption in local, state, and federal government. They saw detailed accounts of the business practices that many tycoons (reporters called them "robber barons") used to squash their competition, control resources, and take over entire industries (including the newspaper business). People read horrifying stories about the dangerous conditions in factories and mills. Photographs showed the reality of big-city problems—child labor, disease, fire, filth, overcrowded tenements. Problems that many Americans had never seen and many city dwellers avoided looking at.

Those reports and articles were disturbing, and there were so many of them. Imagine readers' reactions. People in homes and workplaces and clubs and churches began asking challenging questions. Why did such problems exist? Who was responsible for these issues? Was it possible that the business tycoons most Americans admired weren't the heroes everyone thought they were? And were their own comfortable lives in danger?

Americans everywhere also learned about workers going on strike, walking away from their jobs at mines, mills, and factories to demand better pay and conditions. People read about the terrible violence that often came with those strikes. It was like warfare. Could it spread to any town? And the quotes from speeches given by some labor union leaders sounded like calls for a complete change in America's system of government. Calls for violent revolution. It was frightening.

But what could ordinary people do about any of it? For young women with education and new freedoms—women like Lillian Wald—that wasn't an idle question. They wanted real answers.

In 1889, Lillian found an answer on a visit to her sister. Julia was expecting her first baby and became suddenly ill. A doctor came to the house and asked Lillian to go get a nearby nurse who could stay with Julia while she needed care. Professional nursing was fairly new at the time—the first nursing school in the US had opened in 1872. Most people, including Lillian, had had little or no contact with nurses. They didn't really know what nurses did. But when Lillian saw this woman's skill and efficiency in treating Julia, she recognized it as "serious, definite work." Work she could find fulfilling.

Lillian Wald didn't know that her interest in nursing would lead her to become part of a nationwide push to fix the problems that worried so many Americans. To address the conditions that reporters exposed. To ease the "widespread feeling of unrest and brooding revolution"[5] that frightened middle-class men and women.

She probably wasn't yet aware that thousands of Americans were stepping up to do the enormous work of "reform"—solving problems beyond their personal lives. Most of these reformers were middle class, and an amazing number of them were women. Some worked as individuals, while others organized groups. Across the country, they tackled the real-life issues facing industrial America, issues such as poor housing, poverty, dangerous working conditions, corruption, and more. Some worked out of genuine concern for their fellow Americans. Some worked out of fear that without reform, the nation would fall into revolution or civil war. Whatever their motives were, these people worked to improve American society and to modify—but not overthrow—its economy and government. These reformers became known as "progressives."

Progressives weren't an organization. They weren't a political party—not at first. There were no membership cards or dues to pay, no logo or official name, and no one leader. They were Democrats, Republicans, some socialists, and a lot of people who didn't think of themselves in political terms at all. They did not promote "ideologies"—political ideas and philosophies. Instead, they were "pragmatists." They looked for practical solutions to real problems.

The majority of progressives were white and Protestant, which reflected the majority of Americans at the time. But Black Americans, Native Americans, Catholics, Jews, and other communities pushed for reforms as well. Often, these diverse groups refused to welcome one another into their circles. In fact, many white progressives actively supported segregation (separating groups of people by race, religion, or ethnicity).

And progressives didn't always agree on what needed to be done or how to do it. They didn't even define "progress" the same way. But they did all share some important beliefs and characteristics.

First, progressives believed that American society could change for the better (though they didn't define that the same way). And they believed that society could change without a revolution or a new kind of government. Second, they believed that scientific methods and professional training were key to finding solutions to society's problems. Third, progressives were very strongly committed to their communities. They believed that government—city or "municipal," state, and federal—had to become more active. Government had to promote the "common good"—things that made life better or safer or fairer for all. What the Constitution called promoting the "general welfare."

Progressives didn't do many of the things that we often think of as heroic. They didn't go into physical battle. They didn't explore a dangerous wilderness or defeat evil single-handedly. Most of them worked without drama or fame. They received no medals or citations. Yet, with perseverance, they changed the United States. They modified the US government and the country's economic system. They widened the way Americans thought about their government's responsibilities and about their own duties to one another. They expanded ideas about democracy and opportunity and what it means to be a good citizen.

How did they do all that? For one thing, individual progressives did not wait for anyone else to solve the problems they saw. They jumped in to do it themselves and found like-minded people to work with them. And they relied on facts, persuasion, hands-on hard work, and dogged, tireless, relentless persistence.

These hopeful, dedicated people, Lillian Wald among them, accomplished so much between about 1890 and 1920 that those decades are now known as the Progressive Era.

CHAPTER 4

★★★

Intersections

Less than two years after Lillian Wald first saw a path to "serious, definite work," she completed her courses at the New York Hospital Training School for Nurses in Manhattan. In early 1893, she started taking classes at a medical college in order to learn even more. She also volunteered to teach hygiene and home health care for a group of immigrant women in the Lower East Side.

On a dreary, damp day in March, about six weeks after New Yorkers had read all about Mrs. Astor's exclusive ball, Lillian went to teach her hygiene class. She was showing the women how to make a bed properly when the classroom door opened. Wald looked up and saw a little girl whose face showed a kind of fear that needed no words.

"Your mother is sick. Is that it?" she asked softly.[1] The child nodded. The mother had attended an earlier hygiene class and was pregnant. Wald knew there was trouble. She grabbed a pile of sheets, told her students to go home, and took the little girl's hand.

The two rushed into the misty chill of the crowded, noisy street. Lillian followed the child through a maze of carts and horses, wagons filled with produce, stalls selling fish, children playing, babies crying, vendors shouting . . . How could the little girl even know where she was going? But Wald had to hurry to keep up, as the child didn't hesitate. Lillian lifted her skirts and stepped around foul-smelling piles of garbage, trying to avoid the worst of the horse manure and mud. As she later described it, "the streets were a market-place, unregulated, unsupervised, unclean."[2]

Young Lillian Wald in her nurse's uniform

Finally, the girl came to the door of a tall, shabby, old building just like dozens of other shabby, old buildings. Their fire escapes were filled with all sorts of things the small apartments couldn't hold. The child went through the door, down a hall, and out another door. Lillian followed her into a small, muddy courtyard. They hurried past reeking, doorless outhouses and up slick stairs to an apartment at the back of the building. Its windows opened onto those foul toilets. This was the family's home.

The overwhelming sights and sounds and smells of the street and the courtyard faded as Lillian stared at the small, unlit space and at the other children in front of her—the girl's siblings, she guessed. One room in the apartment was a kitchen, but the sink had no faucets, meaning there was no running water. There was no bathroom, either. The room with windows was a parlor, though the family must have also used it for sleeping and eating and more. Wald felt no comforting heat on this cold day.

The child who'd been so brave in finding help for her mother lived here with her family of seven. Several other people gave the family money in return for space to sleep on the hard floor at night. That money helped the family pay the rent, but it meant that ten or more people crammed together in these small rooms, night after night.

Picture that apartment. Eight big steps in one direction and four big steps in the other. That was how long and wide the entire apartment was. Think of ten or twelve people *living* in that space. Using an outhouse along with dozens of other people from all the overcrowded apartments in the building, sharing the one water spigot in the courtyard. Cold water only.

New York City tenement, 1900

The little girl's mother lay on a worn bed, too weak to move and covered in dried blood. The stench of it was enough to make anyone sick. She'd given birth two days earlier and there had been problems. Had they called for a doctor? Yes, and he had come. But when the family couldn't pay in advance, he left without helping. What? It was a horrible thought. A doctor, whose entire job was to provide medical care, had left a newborn and a bleeding woman because she couldn't pay him.

Lillian thought she'd seen poverty—the poor people waiting in line to see a doctor at the clinic, the women in her home health class. But she hadn't been in the places where those people *lived*.

She hadn't known what their lives were like. Nothing in her own life—not her homelife, schooling, training, or volunteer work—had prepared her for this. Still, she wasn't going to turn away like that doctor had. She wasn't going to run.

Lillian went to work, cleaning the woman and trying to make her comfortable. She put the fresh sheets she'd brought with her on the bed. Then she scrubbed the blood from the floor and cooked the small amount of food she found. The children's father, injured and unable to keep his factory job, was out begging and selling trinkets on the street.[3] He'd be home soon. Lillian promised to come back and wished that she could help—really help—this family. But how? And what about all the other families in the building? And in all the other buildings?

Wald wondered how she hadn't known about this kind of poverty and overcrowding. Why were these people so poor even when they had jobs? What kind of person owned such buildings? Did people in New York's better neighborhoods know about this? They certainly knew about Mrs. Astor's life. But what about life in this tenement? What about all the other tenements?

Lillian later called this experience her "baptism of fire," her "awakening." Her life changed that day. She wrote:

> A sick woman in a squalid rear tenement, so wretched and so pitiful that, in all the years since, I have not seen anything more appealing [sympathetic], determined me, within half an hour, to live on the East Side.[4]

As she lay in bed on the night of her tenement experience, Lillian thought logically about what she could do to keep the kind of health crisis she had witnessed from happening again. By morning, she had a plan.

The first step was to quit her medical school classes. They weren't going to be useful for what she had in mind. The next was to find another nurse to work with her. She thought of Mary Brewster, a good friend from nursing school. Brewster would make a great partner for the work ahead.

Wald told her friend about her plan. They would move into a tenement apartment in the Lower East Side and offer health care and health education to the people in the neighborhood.

Live there? Actually *live* in one of those tenements? Yes.

Lillian was certain that becoming part of the neighborhood was the only way to get to know the people and understand their lives and problems. Most New Yorkers thought of the Lower East Side as horribly overcrowded and filled with crime and disease. They weren't wrong about that. But Wald believed they were mistaken in thinking that the Lower East Side's residents were entirely responsible for their own problems. Or that they were all undesirable immigrants who didn't speak English, couldn't read or write, and didn't know how to raise children. That they didn't have the gumption to pull themselves up in the world.

The Lower East Side residents Wald had met in her hospital work weren't dirty or stupid or lazy. And even if they had been, they didn't deserve to live in squalor. The tenement woman who had been so unwell was clearly "sensitive" to her circumstances. She and her children were polite and grateful for Lillian's help. Wald hadn't seen any evidence at all that the children in that apartment weren't loved or weren't taught right from wrong or how to behave with good manners. They were just poor. And surely, even the children of someone who didn't work hard shouldn't have to live in such hopeless circumstances. What future would they have?

As for being illiterate, at least 75 percent of the immigrants who came to the United States in the late 1800s could read and write in their own languages.[5] Lillian wouldn't have known those numbers, but she would have seen the stands selling newspapers published in Russian, Italian, Yiddish, Chinese, and other languages. And many immigrant men in the neighborhood were skilled craft workers. It might take time, but they could move up in society if they had any opportunity. Earlier immigrants from other countries had done just that. Now, many of their descendants looked down on immigrants. The newcomers in the Lower East Side didn't need gumption—they already had it. What they needed was clean water and fresh air, access to health care and a chance to succeed.

Lillian explained to Mary Brewster that if she could persuade other nurses to join them, they could bring care to people in their homes. After all, that was where the sick people were. Nurses could treat common illnesses before they became serious. They could see to injuries that didn't require surgery. They could offer advice on preventing illnesses, too. And they could assist new mothers. In their home countries, most of those young women

Lillian Wald *(left)* and Mary Brewster *(right)* in hospital uniforms, 1893

would have relied on their own mothers or sisters and aunts for help. But that support was thousands of miles away. Nurses could fill the gap. This practice was already in place in Great Britain. The women there were known as "district nurses." In New York, Lillian would call them "visiting nurses."

Brewster agreed to join Wald. The next step was to find money and a place to live so they could get started. Lillian had a possible benefactor in mind—someone she could rely on for financial support. Betty Loeb, the wife of a very successful banker, was living proof that not every wealthy person spent all their time partying and showing off their money. Loeb felt a sense of responsibility for those less fortunate. She had provided the funds for the home health classes Lillian had volunteered to teach. Perhaps Mrs. Loeb would do the same for the visiting nurses.

Lillian visited Mrs. Loeb at her impressive town house. Heavy, carefully crafted drapes shaded tall windows in the beautifully decorated parlor. Fine oil paintings, several of them family portraits, covered the walls. Betty Loeb often sat in this lovely room and listened to pleas for money. But she was careful with her donations and didn't give to just anyone or anything.

Most people who approached Betty Loeb for money used her donations for charity—money that would help the poor buy food or clothing or fuel for heat. Loeb expected Miss Wald to do the same thing. But Lillian surprised her.

Wald jumped right into her proposal for a visiting nurse service. Mrs. Loeb quickly realized that Lillian Wald didn't simply plan to hand people money or baskets of food. That kind of charity was useful and needed. But Lillian Wald wanted to transform the circumstances that made charity necessary in the first place. No one else had ever said anything about actually changing the way people lived. They didn't discuss ideas for ending poverty or improving the people's health in economically poor communities. Lillian did.

Even more surprising, the young nurse with soft, dark hair and serious eyes spoke of the poor as real people. Individual human beings. She described the woman who lay bleeding with her newborn as having the same hopes and ambitions and feelings as people who had plenty of money. That was an unusual attitude in the late nineteenth century (and still is in some places today).

Loeb found the young woman quite out of the ordinary. She told her daughter that Wald was "either crazy or a genius."[6] In any case, Betty Loeb wanted to help. She would be happy to contribute money to this promising plan. More important, she would introduce Lillian to her daughter's husband, Jacob Schiff.

Schiff had become a giant in the financial world, organizing enormous business deals, particularly in the railroad industry. He could be harsh in his business practices. But like his mother-in-law, Schiff believed in "tzedakah"—the Jewish concept of helping the less fortunate as a religious duty. It was an obligation he took very seriously.

Lillian wore her best business clothes to meet with Schiff in his wood-paneled downtown office. Jacob Schiff was twenty years older than Wald and was a German-Jewish immigrant like her parents and grandparents. He had perfect posture and a carefully trimmed silver beard and mustache, and he wore a finely tailored suit. His eyes were like steel. Lillian said later, "I was nervous, feeling like an inexperienced young girl." But once she started talking about her plans, she gained confidence.[7]

Jacob Schiff liked to invest in the future, in solutions. Lillian Wald's proposal was exactly the kind of thing he thought worth putting money into. He agreed to give Lillian and Mary a monthly donation so they wouldn't have to worry about paying rent or buying food and supplies. And, he told them, they could

Jacob Schiff *(right)* and wife, around 1918

ask for more money if they needed it. He would help with the funds that would keep their work going.[8]

Newspaper society pages generally focused on wealthy New Yorkers' parties, mansions, and balls. All that glamour sold papers. But Schiff knew many of New York's "philanthropists"—people who used their money to make life better for others. He would give Wald the names of some of these potential donors. However, Lillian would have to approach these people on her own. Jacob Schiff preferred to remain anonymous.

Lillian couldn't have wished for better benefactors than Loeb and Schiff. They were willing to share their time and knowledge as well as their money. She happily accepted their offers. Now, she had to prove that her idea of a visiting nurse service would make a real difference.

Lillian Wald and Mary Brewster didn't need an office or clinic, since they would visit people in their homes. But they did need a place to live in the Lower East Side. It wouldn't be large or fancy. That much was certain. But there was one condition. Lillian and Mary agreed that their new home *must* have a bathroom of its own. They couldn't safely care for sick people all day if they couldn't take a bath or wash their hands regularly. Sanitation was vital.

Apartments with bathrooms were rare in the Lower East Side. Try as they might, Wald and Brewster couldn't find a place that met their needs. So after a few months of looking, the two women moved into the College Settlement in July 1893.

"Settlement houses" had started in England about ten years earlier. Small groups of college students and young college graduates came together to live in an impoverished neighborhood, learn about its people, and offer services to them. The settlement house plan reached the United States by 1886 and was spreading quickly (in 1897 there were seventy-four settlements in the US; by 1910, that number was about four hundred across the country). But most Americans didn't know much about the idea in the early 1890s.

Each settlement house chose its own focus. Many followed the model of Jane Addams's Hull House in Chicago. Founded in 1890, Hull House offered immigrants classes in English and citizenship, and helped newcomers adjust to life in America. Some, like College Settlement (founded in 1889), offered students the opportunity to study sociology and economics while gathering data on child labor, tenement life, and more. The information went to New York's commissions on housing and labor. Other settlements focused on the arts—music, drama, fine arts—and provided lessons, classes, space, and supplies to people living in the neighborhood. Many immigrants brought their own skills and cultural traditions to the settlement programs.

Wald's desire to improve health care for the poor wasn't part of College Settlement's work. But she and Mary could stay there while they continued to search for their own quarters. Lillian watched and learned how the settlement house operated, and made use of her new knowledge as she moved forward.

A few months later, in September, Wald and Brewster found a tenement apartment with a bathroom on Jefferson Street. Lillian was twenty-six years old by then, but her German Jewish parents and Brewster's Irish Catholic parents worried about their daughters' plans. Why did the two young women have to be so unconventional? It would be much easier if they just settled down to marriage and family. Despite their worry, both sets of parents donated furniture from their homes and gifts of a small heater and kitchen equipment for the apartment. Grateful and relieved, Lillian and Mary settled in. Their timing couldn't have been better.

The American economy had fallen into an economic depression (called a "panic" at the time) over the summer of 1893. Factories and mills shut down. Many stores closed. Banks went out of business. People everywhere lost jobs or saw their wages cut. Many lost their savings and their homes. In the Lower East Side, health problems worsened as already serious poverty increased. Doctor visits were beyond what anyone could afford. But Lillian and Mary faced challenges in trying to offer help.

Most of the residents of the Jefferson Street building were

Wald *(left)* and Jane Adams *(right)*, 1916

Jewish immigrants from Romania or Russia and didn't speak English. Communication was difficult for the nurses. And immigrants were often afraid of medical professionals or ashamed to ask for help since they couldn't pay for it. Lillian and Mary would have to earn their trust.

Fortunately, the motherly woman who took care of the building in exchange for a free basement apartment happily stepped in to help Wald and Brewster. The tenants knew and trusted Mrs.

McRae, an Irish immigrant. If she said the nurses were good people, the other tenants believed her. And they spread the word to people in nearby tenements.

Lillian and Mary soon spent their days climbing down the stairs from their fifth-floor apartment into the noisy, bustling streets around them. They visited their clients in other tenements, climbing the stairs to their apartments. When they finished with one sick person, they climbed back down the stairs and moved on to the next person who needed help. They often climbed forty or fifty flights of stairs in a day. It was exhausting. But in addition to tending to sick people, Lillian tried to meet every family in every building they visited. She wanted to see what their everyday situations were like. And she thought that if they met her, they'd be more willing to ask for help when they needed it.

She and Mary looked at the causes of each family's troubles, too. They made sure people understood how to use their medicines. They sometimes loaned money to those who couldn't afford a prescription. They negotiated with doctors who refused to see patients who couldn't pay right away. And they helped families get food, job referrals, assistance with translations of documents, and the like.

With Jacob Schiff's advice, Lillian also learned how to raise money. It seemed she'd actually learned some useful skills as a young woman in Rochester. All those teas and socials had taught her how to behave at fancy dinners and in fancy homes. She could talk comfortably to upper-class men and women. Her good taste and fondness for fine clothes came in handy too. She could dress appropriately when she visited a wealthy home or attended an event. Whether they knew it or not, the wealthy were more likely to listen to someone in fine clothing.

Wald's "magnetic" personality helped as well.[9] When Lillian cornered a wealthy potential donor, she never actually asked for money. Instead, she described how hard the visiting nurses worked and how she wished she could hire more nurses. She told stories of hardworking people who had fallen on difficult times. She let her dinner partners know about the challenges of affording medicines.[10] As one wealthy man joked, it cost $5,000 to sit next to Lillian Wald at the dining table.[11]

Soon, Wald and Brewster had become so successful that they needed more space to house more nurses. They needed a place where Lillian's ideas for wider services could become reality. By 1895, she and Jacob Schiff had formed a real partnership in what Lillian and Mary now called the Visiting Nurse Service. Schiff was ready to support this next step.

Then and Now: Philanthropists

Then: The millionaires of the late 1800s were like all human beings—complicated. Many used their wealth to show off or to make even more wealth. Others, like Jacob Schiff, chose to use much of their wealth to make society better for everyone. They were known as philanthropists.

John D. Rockefeller was worth over $400 billion in today's money. But Rockefeller described men who worked just to accumulate more and more money as "despicable." He lived very well, but not in the gaudy, obvious manner that so many millionaires of his time did. And he believed in using his wealth for good.

Like Jacob Schiff, Rockefeller's religion—he was a Baptist—played a big part in his charitable giving. He believed in investing in institutions that would allow individuals to improve themselves. He wrote, "What most people seek cannot be bought with money."[12]

Rockefeller founded the University of Chicago in 1890. In 1901, he created the Rockefeller Institute for Medical Research. Soon after came other organizations focused on education and city sanitation. He also established the Rockefeller Foundation, an organization that has given over $22 billion to support health, sustainable energy, education, the arts, and more.[13]

Andrew Carnegie also used his wealth to benefit those who wanted to improve themselves. He published an essay in 1889 that became known as "The Gospel of Wealth." He described his belief that the wealthy should use their riches for good—for helping the poor to help themselves. "The man who dies thus rich dies disgraced," he said.[14]

Carnegie gave huge sums to colleges, hospitals, concert halls, parks, and more. Like Rockefeller, he established foundations to continue his giving long after he was gone. And he built public libraries across the country and in Europe—more than 2,500 libraries in all. Many of them are considered to be among the most beautiful buildings in the US. By the time he died in 1919, Carnegie had given away more than 90 percent of his fortune.

Men like Schiff, Rockefeller, and Carnegie didn't believe in handouts. They believed in giving people opportunities to help themselves. With schools and libraries, people without much money could still become educated. Good health care could mean steadier work. Public parks and the arts offered ways to feed the soul.

But it was up to the individual to take advantage of what was offered.

This is where the philanthropists of the late 1800s get complicated. Their philanthropy fit the image of "captains of industry." They saw themselves as financing a better society. But the way they made their fortunes fit the image of "robber barons." They had risen to the top using what many people consider unethical, immoral, and sometimes illegal means. And the men who worked such long hours for them in dreadful conditions had no time to visit a library or attend school.

Tycoon philanthropists also ignored how much labor had changed since they had their first jobs. They insisted that anyone could do what they had done, even as their own policies kept most of their workers from getting ahead.

Now: Today's billionaires are just as complicated as the millionaires of the Gilded Age. According to the *Bloomberg Billionaires Index*, Elon Musk—CEO of Tesla and SpaceX—was worth $434 billion and was the world's richest man in 2025.[15] He is on track to become the world's first trillionaire. *Forbes* magazine reported that Musk has given away less than 1 percent of his wealth.

On the other hand, Bill Gates, co-founder of Microsoft and worth over $120 billion in 2025, established a foundation to address issues of poverty and disease around the world. Today it is one of the world's largest charitable foundations. Much of its funding comes from Warren Buffett, founder of Berkshire Hathaway. In 2025, Buffett was worth $148 billion. He has given away nearly 50 percent of his wealth and has plans to give away most of the rest of his money. He has encouraged other billionaires to pledge their fortunes to charity as well.[16]

And so: The numbers present us with a lot of questions. Do the very wealthy have an obligation to give money to charity? Would industrialists like Andrew Carnegie have been more effective in ending poverty and other ills if they had used their wealth to pay their workers higher wages and provide them with better working conditions? Would the very wealthy of today be more effective if they paid more in taxes than they currently do (the average US billionaire pays a smaller percent of their income in taxes than the average wage-earning American does)? Do employees or the government or anyone else have the right to tell billionaire business owners what to do with their money? And can anyone then or now earn millions of dollars entirely on their own?

Experts disagree on the answers to these questions. But the questions were worth thinking about in 1900 and are still worth thinking about today.

CHAPTER 5

★★★

The House on Henry Street

On a summer morning in 1895, Lillian Wald and Mary Brewster packed their bags and supplies and moved to a house at 265 Henry Street, just blocks from their Jefferson Street apartment. Jacob Schiff had purchased the old redbrick house for the Visiting Nurses. The building was solid, with a wide front door, lovely windows, and a backyard. It had been beautiful once and could be again.

Wald soon had more than a dozen nurses on her team. Several lived at the Henry Street Settlement, while others lived in nearby tenements. A variety of donors covered their living expenses and a small salary. And some nurses were happy to volunteer their services without pay.

The new members of the Henry Street "family" learned from Lillian to look beyond a patient's medical needs. Wald insisted that they pay attention to the condition of the home, the food a family had or didn't have, the cleanliness of the rooms, beds, and children. Were the children going to school? Were they working? Did the family have an income? Lillian knew that all these factors were connected. The nurses also learned to keep detailed records for every person and family. And they figured out that walking across

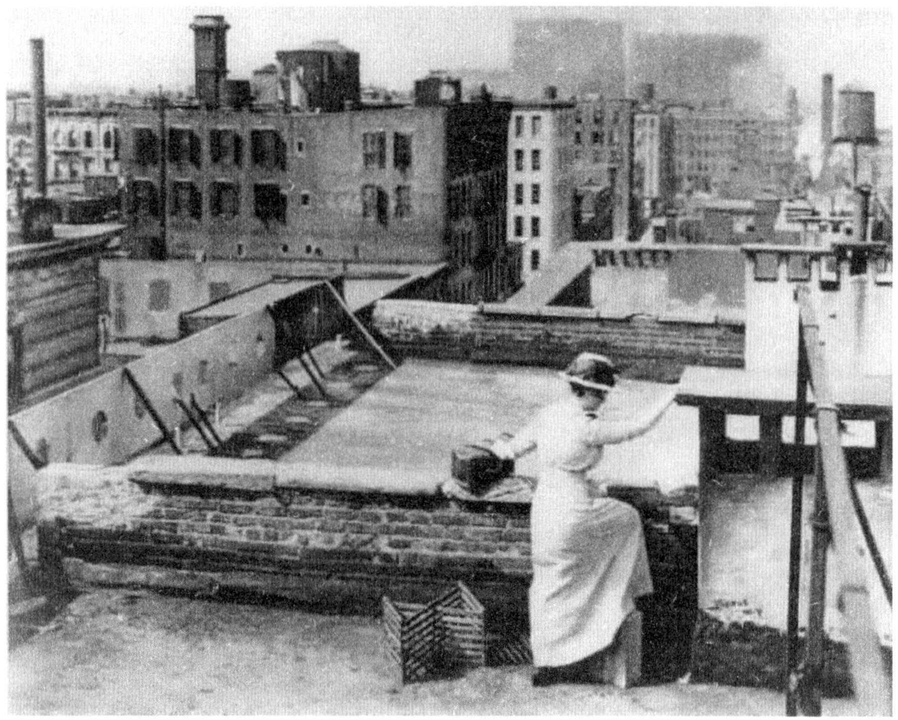

Henry Street nurse climbing over a rooftop

rooftops from one building to the next saved a lot of time, energy, and steps.

Lillian provided her nurses with uniforms and medical bags. She wanted them to look professional, and they did. But gaining the trust of neighborhood residents was still a challenge. Wald thought that badges of some sort might help by identifying her organization in an official way.

When she met the president of the New York City Board of Health at a social event, Lillian described the work she and the other nurses were doing. He was impressed. She then asked if the city board might provide a badge the nurses could wear to identify themselves.

Several people who knew her described Lillian as the kind of person no one could say no to—whether she was asking for badges or big donations. Apparently, those descriptions were accurate. The nurses soon had badges stating that they were under the "auspices" (sponsorship) of the Board of Health. Lillian was delighted, especially since the Visiting Nurse Service received no money from the board and had no board supervision. But the badges showed that city health officials took the nurses' work seriously.

Visiting Nurse Service of New York badge

Wald continued to visit patients and their families. But she also spent time finding solutions to the problems that contributed to poor health. For one thing, neighborhood children had no safe place to run and play, to get some sun. They needed a playground where they could build muscle and stamina. Older children needed a place that would keep them out of trouble.

Soon after moving to the Henry Street Settlement, Lillian got permission to use the yard at the school next door in addition to her own yard. Later she was able to add the yard on the other side of hers. She raised money for playground equipment and a garden. The place became "a heaven of delight" used by young children in the morning and schoolchildren in the afternoon. When Wald added hanging Japanese lanterns for lighting, young adults came to talk and sing together in the evenings.[1]

Next, Lillian worked to get the children to the countryside. Most of them had never left the Lower East Side. They'd never been to Central Park, less than five miles from Henry Street. They'd never been to any park. They'd never seen a forest or a farm. They didn't know what cows or sheep looked or sounded like. As Lillian recorded later, one child who went with a Henry

Street group to a stage production of *Peter Pan* thought the crocodile was a field mouse.[2] Try to imagine knowing nothing about the world outside a single neighborhood. Wald believed that these children needed to experience nature for their mental and intellectual health.

Lillian turned to her growing list of donors. But instead of seeking money, she asked those who owned nearby country houses to open those homes to the children. The request was much more personal than making a donation, but once again, almost no one could say no to Lillian Wald. Think of the magic those trips were for a boy or girl who had no idea that green fields or woods or ponds and lakes even existed. Why wasn't the

Playground at Henry Street

city spending tax money on those needs? Building playgrounds or recreation centers? Why weren't schoolchildren going on field trips to the countryside?

Many taxpayers in the late 1800s and early 1900s didn't see child welfare or other kinds of services as government responsibilities. Mayors and city leaders agreed. But if services were not a government responsibility, whose responsibility were they? Who owns a city? It's an odd question, but think about it. Does everyone who lives there own the city? Maybe it's everyone who lives there and pays taxes. Or everyone who owns property in the city. Or perhaps it's the businesses that create jobs and bring money into the city.

Lillian Wald didn't try to answer that question. She might not have thought about it. Most people don't. But Wald did think a lot about children's needs. Those needs had to be met.

The Henry Street Settlement offered lessons in English and in skills such as sewing and embroidery. Volunteers led clubs for young boys, for young girls, for older boys, older girls, and adults. Each club focused on a different hobby or interest, from history to drama to nature study to woodworking, and much more. And whether they were children or adults, club members wrote their own rules and governed themselves.

"Nursing is only the beginning," Wald said.[3] She had a lot of ideas for serving the people of the Lower East Side. But she needed support and suggestions from all sorts of people from all walks of life. Men and women, business owners, working people, government officials. She began hosting dinner parties and invited her guests to discuss their ideas as well as hers for meeting the community's needs.

Lillian's parties, of course, were nothing like the parties Mrs. Astor hosted. There were no gold-plated forks or uniformed waiters at the Henry Street Settlement. Wald herself served the simple but good food. That was a real treat for residents of the Lower East Side. Wealthy and famous people looked forward to an invitation too.

Picture millionaire Jacob Schiff in his finely fitted suit and silk tie sitting next to a tailor whose own jacket was worn and whose hands showed years of hard work. It was part of Wald's plan. She liked and respected Schiff, but she knew that he still held on to old ideas about people being poor through their own fault. Lillian knew how different these two men were. But she also knew that they both had a deep commitment to their Jewish faith. Sure enough, after some tension and an argument about workers' strikes, the banker and the tailor got along well. They had a lot to talk about—some of it in Hebrew.

265 Henry Street

Schiff was a frequent dinner guest at Henry Street. Over time, his views softened, just as Lillian had hoped. Getting to know people as individual human beings instead of seeing faceless crowds often has that effect.[4]

Jacob Riis, a Danish immigrant who gained fame as a photographer and investigative journalist, came to dinner now and then too. His magazine articles and bestselling book, *How the Other Half Lives*, showed Americans the conditions of life in the Lower East Side. Riis photographed children sleeping in doorways and whole families working in dim, dirty, windowless rooms. People using rags for mattresses. Young boys and girls in factories working barefoot on huge, dangerous machines. Page after page of the grim reality in too many Americans' lives. Surely, if people knew how difficult life was for their neighbors, they would demand change. Wouldn't they?

Riis and Wald became good friends. They worked together to support government involvement in tenement housing reform and in building city parks and playgrounds.

Riis also introduced Lillian Wald to his friend Theodore Roosevelt. Roosevelt was New York City's police commissioner at the time and a progressive. He, too, accepted invitations to the Henry Street dinners and was happy to meet neighborhood residents and hear their concerns. Roosevelt was interested in Lillian's work and counted her as a friend. They remained friends

Theodore Roosevelt, NYC police commissioner, around 1895

when he was elected New York's governor and then vice president of the United States. After President William McKinley was assassinated in 1900 and Roosevelt became president, he continued to support Wald and her ideas for lifting children out of poverty. He even invited her to the White House to discuss the government's responsibility to children.

Plenty of politicians in both political parties opposed progressive ideas. The government had never been involved in child welfare or health care and the like. Government had never regulated businesses, for the most part. Many politicians believed that none of that was government's job. Others opposed progressive reforms in order to keep their wealthy industrialist supporters happy. But several politicians had expanded their definition of government responsibility the way Wald had expanded her definition of the domestic sphere. Theodore Roosevelt was among them. So were a number of officials at the local and state levels. Voters—only men at the time—would have to decide who was right.

Lillian Wald continued to visit patients, manage the nurses, host dinners, raise funds, and more. All the while, she kept careful records and sent regular reports to Jacob Schiff and to the New York City Board of Health. Those records were important as Wald worked to persuade the city to hire school nurses. She used her data to argue that nurses in schools could help limit the spread of disease, treat simple things like head lice that kept children out of school, and improve school attendance. In 1902, New York became the first city in the country to employ school nurses. Attendance improved, the number of illnesses declined, and other cities soon followed New York's lead.[5]

Lillian's data helped in seeking city funds to supply clean, fresh milk to poor children, and in other projects too. But the records were more than statistics. More than numbers. Wald showed government officials and the wealthy that the people of the Lower East Side were living, breathing individuals. She put a human face on communities and people who had been ignored.

Lillian wrote about visiting a neighborhood shoemaker named Michael. She arrived at his door just as the family was sitting down to eat. Sitting with them was a man she had not seen before. Neither had Michael's family. The man was a stranger who had just been released from prison. Who would bring a person like that home to eat with his family? Michael explained quietly that the man was hungry and the day was bitter cold. "We must chance it," he said. "It's no weather for a man like that to be on the streets."[6]

Another man, a widower with two children, was lucky enough to have a job in the midst of the deep financial depression. He didn't make much money, but he took in his cousin and her two children while her husband was in the hospital. He had also invited the family of a friend who had died to live in the small apartment. And on most nights, he insisted that another family in the building come over for dinner. He didn't know that family at all when he first asked them to dine with him, but he knew the father was out of work. Somehow, he fed all these people day after day.[7]

Lillian's stories went on and on. These kindnesses included a Jewish woman trying to find a priest for her dying neighbor who was Catholic. Poor families taking in neighbors' babies when their mothers died. The kindnesses were enormous. But the needs were even greater.

Eventually, Lillian reached the same conclusion other progressives did. No charity, no settlement house, no number of volunteers could solve the growing problems America's cities faced at the start of the twentieth century. Government would have to step in—local government, state government, even the federal government. Volunteers couldn't force Mr. Astor to make his tenements safe. Charities couldn't insist that parents send their children to school. Good intentions couldn't make sure that a city's water was clean. It was time for government to live up to the US Constitution's preamble and "promote the general welfare" of the American people.

Lillian Wald cared for all kinds of people in the Lower East Side. But her mind and heart were always with the children of the neighborhood. When she visited President Theodore Roosevelt in Washington, Wald pointed out that the government had sent the secretary of agriculture to the South to study the problem of the boll weevil—a beetle that was destroying cotton plants. Surely the government could also study and find a solution to the poverty that was destroying children across the country.[8] Roosevelt couldn't say no to Lillian Wald, and he didn't want to. But Congress wasn't ready to pass such a measure. Finally, the next president, William Howard Taft, got a bill through the House of Representatives and the Senate. The Children's Bureau opened in 1912.

Lillian Wald always had more to do. She and Jacob Riis worked with New York City's park commissioner to establish the Outdoor Recreation League in 1898. They raised money to build the first permanent, city-funded playground in the United States. Over twenty thousand children flooded into Seward Park on opening day.[9]

Wald campaigned to end child labor, to shut down sweatshops, to provide specialized education for disabled children, to expand protections for factory workers, and much more. She welcomed people of all ethnicities, all faiths, and all races

Lillian Ward (age fifty-two) painting, 1919

to the Henry Street Settlement. Her openness to people of all backgrounds was extraordinary in the United States in the early twentieth century. So was Wald's 1909 participation in organizing the National Association for the Advancement of Colored People—the NAACP—dedicated to ending racial segregation and discrimination. Wald signed the group's founding document and hosted the organizers' opening reception at the Henry Street Settlement.[10]

In 1913, the Visiting Nurse Service celebrated twenty years of work in the Lower East Side with a pageant and parade on Henry Street. The city finally paved the broken, muddy street for the event. Thousands of residents watched from windows, rooftops, and fire escapes. At least ten thousand more people filled the sidewalks. Hundreds of men, women, and children from the settlement's clubs and classes, past and present, gathered to march to the house on Henry Street. Wald watched from a grandstand, surrounded by the mayor, government officials, benefactors, friends, and fellow reformers (sadly, Mary Brewster had died of heart disease in 1901). When the visiting nurses marched together down Henry Street and faced the grandstand, thousands upon thousands of people of every background cheered Lillian Wald. One person described Henry Street that day as "flooded with love."[11]

By that time, the Henry Street Settlement had expanded to nearly one hundred nurses who made close to two hundred thousand nursing visits in one year.[12] With the help of donations, Wald had acquired three more buildings on Henry Street in addition to the house at 265. She had opened branches of the service in several other parts of New York City too. They served neighborhoods where most residents were Black, neighborhoods where most people were of one ethnic background or another, and mixed neighborhoods. Through it all, Henry Street remained the center of activity. In one month alone, some twenty-five thousand people came for help or classes or clubs or to work, study, play, or simply visit.

Lillian Wald had earned respect around the country and the world as a nursing professional and as a reformer. She had introduced the term "public health nurse," and her visiting nurses had become the model for a new kind of nursing nationwide. When the State of New York passed a law expanding its Department of Health in 1913, the report noted that "The advent of trained nursing marks not only a new era in the treatment of the sick, but a new era in public health administration."[13]

Henry Street Visiting Nurse Service

It was a new era in other ways too. New York had passed one of the nation's first tenement laws in 1901—something Wald had lobbied for. The law required windows in every room and toilets in every apartment. The buildings that went up after that law passed weren't exactly Mrs. Astor's mansion, but they were a vast improvement over what Lillian Wald had seen in 1893. Child labor and compulsory education laws that were passed just after 1900 had worked to keep children in school and provide them with improved skills when they did enter the workforce. But there was always more to do.

When Wald retired from the Henry Street Settlement in 1933, there were 265 nurses working in the Visiting Nurse Service.[14] But health care was only one piece of the settlement's mission by then.

In 1944, the Visiting Nurse Service broke off from the

Henry Street Settlement and became the Visiting Nurse Service of New York. Now called VNS Health, it is one of the biggest not-for-profit home health organizations in the country.[15]

Even without the nursing service, the Henry Street Settlement continued to grow and serve thousands of people in a variety of ways. Over time, the settlement built a theater for arts programs and performances. The theater was a huge success. Award-winning actors, dancers, directors, and producers taught there (and still do). And several of the neighborhood children who took classes at the theater grew up to become entertainers.

The settlement built a music school as well. It trained thousands of musicians and provided a place for neighborhood residents to perform. The Henry Street Settlement also opened a workshop for furniture and appliance repair, developed senior programs, provided early childhood education, held leadership classes, and much more. Many of the children who benefited from these programs went on to become successful as craftspeople, or in business, medicine, the law, education, and more. The stories go on, proof that Lillian Wald's belief in every person's worth was justified.

As a young woman, Lillian Wald had questioned the idea of a narrow domestic sphere as a woman's only place. Ultimately, she came to see home and family in a different way, an expanded way. The Henry Street Settlement was her home. And though she loved her birth family and stayed close to them (her mother even lived at Henry Street for a time and taught sewing classes), the people of the Henry Street Settlement were her family too.

Wald's "sphere" included the whole Lower East Side and continued to grow. As she believed:

> Each of us is whole and worthy.
> Poverty is a social issue (not an individual failing).
> There is power in bridging differences.
> Neighbors matter.
> In times of need, act.[16]

Other progressive women around the United States, as well as working-class women and men, felt the same way.

CHAPTER 6

★★★

The Homes of Indiana

Albion Fellows Bacon would have cared about the poor neighborhoods near her home in Evansville, Indiana, if she'd known they existed. But she was careful *not* to know. When Albion went shopping, she went to the nicest stores in the nicest neighborhoods. When she read the newspaper, she skipped any articles about crime or terrible accidents. She'd always wanted to be surrounded by beauty. Now she was a young woman with a husband and small children. She still worked to "exclude every ugly or blighting thing from [her] life."[1] Bacon was certain that there was nothing she could do about any of it.[2] She didn't read about politics, either. The political world was just as ugly as dirty streets or shabby businesses. And as a woman, she had absolutely no say in politics.

Albion was born in Evansville in 1865, right as the American Civil War was ending. Her father—the Reverend Fellows—had died just a few weeks before her birth, leaving her mother with three young daughters. So Mrs. Fellows moved to the nearby village where she'd grown up and where she and her girls could be close to family. McCutchanville was a tiny farming community with no paved streets, no stores, a single church (Methodist), and a one-room schoolhouse. The post office was in the postmaster's living room.

Albion Fellows Bacon, around 1910 or 1915

Bacon wrote later that she had a "sheltered" life. She played with her friends and siblings, went to school and church, wrote poems and plays, and made art. She described her young self as timid, shy, small, and a "born coward" who was afraid of dogs and storms and all sorts of other things. As she grew, she learned to make herself face her fears—even her fear of the big dog that barked and growled every time she walked by. But new anxieties always seemed to replace the old ones.[3] Even so, she had a mostly happy childhood filled with love, the beautiful countryside, and the security of having enough to eat and a decent place to live.

The family moved back to Evansville around the time Albion started high school. An excellent student and very competitive, she graduated in just two years. She hoped to go to college as her older sisters had, and she wanted to study art. But her mother couldn't afford it. There simply wasn't enough money. Instead, a terribly disappointed Albion went to work as a secretary in her uncle's law office. Rather than learning to draw and paint, she learned to write down exactly what someone said as quickly as they said it in a style known as shorthand. She learned to read dry, detailed legal documents, and to walk into a courthouse—something few women did in those days—with a look of confidence. Albion had no way of knowing that those skills would be very important to her years later.

At twenty-three, Albion Fellows married Hilary Bacon. He was fourteen years older than Albion and the owner of a prosperous dry goods (clothing, fabrics, canned and packaged foods, etc.) store in Evansville. They settled into a big, comfortable house at the edge of town and soon started a family. Life was good. The couple's home had beautiful views of the countryside Albion loved. The Bacons and their neighbors all had big yards with trees and flowers, and they were close to the nicest stores and shops.

Happily busy with her first daughter, as well as her home, nearby friends, and her art, Albion liked the domestic sphere. It never occurred to her to explore interests or activities outside of her role at home, except at church. However, after her second daughter was born in 1892, Bacon suffered from what may have been depression. She was constantly tired and uninterested in doing anything. Even when she eventually recovered her energy and began painting and reading again, she didn't choose to join women's clubs or church groups the way her friends and neighbors did. She told anyone who tried to enlist her in those organizations that she was too busy. And she paid no attention to the changes women like Lillian Wald were making in various parts of the country. Those women looked closely at shabby buildings and dirty streets, what Albion thought of as ugliness. That wasn't for her. Albion Bacon was content with her traditional, quiet, middle-class life. Or so she thought.

One day, Bacon's younger daughter complained that a boy in her class wouldn't leave her alone. Harry wasn't just a pest. He was dirty—so dirty, the child said, that his smell made her sick. Bacon was shocked. If her daughter wasn't exaggerating, something had to be done. The rudeness was one thing. But why was any child coming to school filthy? It wasn't healthy for him or the rest of the children.

Albion went to the school to talk to her daughter's teacher. She saw a number of children like her own—girls as "immaculate as daisies, with shining curls and spotless frocks [dresses]," and boys in clean shirts with their hair still wet from the morning's washing up.[4] But she also saw children whose hair hadn't been washed or brushed in a very long time. Whose clothes were worn and stained and too small or too big. Whose hands were caked in dirt and grime. Children who were too thin.

Bacon forgot all about why she had come to the school. Those children she saw—they needed so much. Where did they live that their parents weren't taking better care of them? Being clean, having clothes that fit, having enough food—those were comforts that Albion and her daughters took for granted.

Bacon kept her girls close as they started for home. She looked around and saw things she'd never noticed before. Part of the schoolyard was covered in sharp, broken rocks. A heap of garbage was piled up behind a nearby market. The boys, one of her daughters told her, liked to throw the rotten food at one another. That was why the girls played in the street on the other side of the school.[5] Bacon could hardly believe it.

That same afternoon, Albion Bacon went to talk to members of the Civic Improvement Association, a group of women who worked with the local government to make Evansville as nice a place to live as possible. They agreed to go with her to see the city attorney and find out if the city owned the empty land next to the shabby playground. If it did, perhaps the school would be able to use the lot for a nicer outdoor space.

Albion had never done anything like this. A big part of her didn't want to be doing it now. She simply wasn't the sort of person who went to city offices to demand anything. But she couldn't let her children—or other people's children—play in that dangerous yard. She told herself that the others in the group could do the talking. They knew how to speak to the city attorney. She would say nothing. Absolutely nothing.

Her plan didn't work. Once they were in the attorney's office and talking about the situation, Bacon jumped into the conversation. She surprised herself. Where was the timid, shy Albion who avoided anything unpleasant? Unfortunately, her newfound courage didn't matter. The city owned the land, but the group didn't get permission to use it. Albion went home, disappointed.

However, the members of the Civic Improvement Association didn't give up. They went on lobbying for the land without Bacon. Eventually, the city agreed to add some of the nearby space to the school grounds and pay for a fence around the new yard. Plans for making the spot somewhere children could safely play got underway.

Albion was pleased to hear the news. But a nice playground would do nothing for the children who came to school dirty with their noses running or lice in their hair. It would do nothing about the student who coughed all day or looked feverish. Or the child who didn't play because constant hunger left her with no energy. Those images disturbed her, yet Bacon didn't see anything she could do, no matter how sorry she felt for the children.

In the meantime, her own children came down with scarlet fever. Albion's daughters suffered with high fevers, throats so sore they couldn't swallow, burning rashes, and more. Today, scarlet fever can be treated with antibiotics. But there were no antibiotics in the late 1800s, and the disease was a leading cause of death in young children.[6] Terrified, Albion watched over her daughters day after day, night after night. They were lucky. Both girls recovered.

Bacon couldn't say for certain that her daughters had caught the fever from their classmates. But it was likely (today we know that scarlet fever and other illnesses, including flu and COVID-19, are spread through tiny droplets released when a person coughs, sneezes, or simply breathes). And she couldn't remain in her domestic sphere, as if the rest of the world didn't affect her own small bubble, any longer. Obviously, it did. Albion went to the Civic Improvement Association again. This time, she was ready to join the group and volunteered to serve on the sanitation committee.[7] Someone had to find ways to keep children at school safe from disease.

Always a good student, Albion Bacon now learned everything she could about sanitation. She would have preferred to study art or literature. But she was determined to find the information she needed to make a difference in local children's health.

Bacon started reading articles about preventing the spread of illnesses. She looked *into* the city's alleys as she walked by instead of turning away. What she saw upset her. Albion forced herself to look anyway, just as she had forced herself to face the big dog that scared her so much as a child. She looked at the trash and slimy puddles. She saw children playing in filth. She didn't know until later that those children didn't just play in the alleys. They *lived* there.[8] Picture that—whole families living in an alley. It was no wonder that children came to school dirty and sick.

Bacon's studies led her to read Jacob Riis's 1890 book *How the Other Half Lives*. The pictures of poverty in New York City tore at her heart and stayed in her mind. Especially photographs of children sleeping in stairwells or working in factories. But New York was a city of three million people in the 1890s. Evansville, Indiana, had only thirty thousand residents. It was a hundred times smaller than New York. Yes, there were spots of poverty in Evansville, but it was nothing like New York City. Or was it?

Evansville may have been tiny compared to New York, but the urban problems Albion saw there were more than enough. She decided to do something beyond reporting what she had learned so that someone else could look for solutions. She wanted to be part of the solutions herself.

Bacon became the first volunteer with the Friendly Visitors Circle—a group of women who made visits to the poor. The Friendly Visitors weren't health care workers like Lillian Wald's visiting nurses. They didn't bring money or food or clothing to the poor as charitable groups did. They simply visited, listened, and treated the poor as they would any other person. The idea was to give people some of the respect and dignity that living in poverty stole from them. The charity of larger organizations could provide money and food and so on. But handouts didn't help people feel their own worth. Visits did. At least, that was what the Friendly Visitors hoped. There's little evidence to show how the people they visited really felt.

Albion went with Caroline Rein, the head of the group, to visit people in a part of Evansville that she had never seen. For that matter, she hadn't known the neighborhood existed. It was the kind of place she had so carefully avoided for years.

The tenement building she visited had been a hospital originally and was a sturdy old structure. But the grounds around the building hadn't been cared for in years. Neither had the building itself. Women and small children filled the front porch, where laundry hung on the railings to air. Inside, the huge hallway was filthy and filled with children, babies, mothers, and a few old men. Each family, Albion learned, had one room here. One room for a whole family.

Bacon thought of the Riis book. The slums of Evansville weren't nearly as densely packed as New York's Lower East Side, but the poverty was just as serious. She felt overwhelmed.

"Seeing!" she wrote later. "The word is too passive. Sights and smells rose and assaulted me, choked and gashed me, and the scars remain yet."[9]

This was Albion Fellows Bacon's awakening. Like Lillian Wald, she was about to become a reformer.

Visiting disadvantaged residents of Evansville was a kind of education that Albion Bacon would never have had in college. Her work taught her to see people living in poverty as individual, real human beings. Like Lillian Wald, Bacon realized that many middle-class and upper-class people at the time believed that people were poor because they lacked the drive or ambition to do better for themselves (some people still think this way today). She soon concluded that this attitude was misguided and mistaken. Albion listened to these people's stories and saw that anyone could fall on hard times. Anyone could lose a job or be widowed with no income. Anyone could become ill and be unable to pay the bills. Even people who did lack ambition may have had plenty of it at one time. But they'd been beaten down. Their children knew only poverty, hunger, and need. None of that meant that the poor were less worthy human beings than other groups of people. They were simply less fortunate or privileged. Not as lucky.

Bacon continued learning as she worked with the Friendly Visitors. After a while, she suggested that the group could be more effective if they invited men as well as women to volunteer as visitors. She recruited her husband, the minister at her church, and a number of other men to become visitors. They could talk to men and older boys in ways the women might not be able to.

Albion was right about what the men could accomplish. They were able to help many of the boys they visited stay in school and out of trouble. They found jobs for some of the unemployed men. But no matter what the visitors did, and no matter how much financial help the charities gave, they couldn't solve the problem of terrible housing. And nothing the Friendly Visitors or the Civic Improvement Society said or did persuaded the owners of the dreary buildings to improve them. There were no laws telling landlords that they had to provide running water or toilets or heat or light or anything else.

"Indiana would have nothing to say if her tenements were built fifty stories high without a single window," Bacon wrote later.[10] That attitude and lack of oversight had to change. But how? Visiting people, listening to them, wasn't enough. It wasn't close to enough when Bacon knew she could go home to a lovely, comfortable house and those people she had visited would still be in dark, damp, unhealthy rooms. She wrote, "Down deep in my heart came a knowledge that I could never rest until I could do something."[11]

CHAPTER 7

Municipal Housekeeping

Albion Bacon now had two more children—twins born in 1901 when their sisters were twelve and nine. She was thrilled with her new son and daughter, but they kept her very busy, even though she and her husband could afford nurses to help care for them. As soon as she was able, however, Albion returned to her volunteer work while the older girls were at school. In fact, her work expanded, and she often took the babies with her in their buggy.

First was the Friendly Visitors. Then, the men's branch of Visitors. Next, Albion learned that young women living on their own faced real dangers right in Evansville. A nurse who worked for the Bacon family came in one evening as pale as a ghost. A man had been following her. Albion thought about all the other young women who faced the same dangers. She went to the newly organized Home Missionary Society at her church. The women there agreed to study the city's darker side. Albion insisted they *really* study all aspects of the situation. Schools, jails, housing—everything. And members must go in person to see conditions for themselves. They must do research and keep records. In other words, they must take a scientific approach.

Horrified at the shabby buildings, dark alleys, and filthy streets that young factory girls had to pass through every day, the women of the society went to work.[1] Albion had awakened a whole new group of people who had been sleepwalking, as she described it. People who had thought that poverty and crime existed in other places, but not in their own city. People who needed to know the reality of life for their fellow citizens if anything was going to be done about it.

The society opened a shelter for women and girls who needed a temporary, safe place to stay. They advertised the shelter in train stations and posted warnings for the young women who came from the country. Many of those young women had never lived in a city before. They didn't know how to watch out for themselves in an urban environment. Soon after that, Bacon learned from a secretary at the Associated Charities office that young women who worked in factories often ate lunch at their machines or went to the rather seedy nearby saloons to eat. Some factory girls didn't eat at all. So Albion and the secretary went into the loud, dusty factories where young workers stood for hours at looms or wheels, or rolled cigars. Bacon had been past the gloomy buildings many times. But she'd never thought about who was inside. Now she wanted to learn everything about these places.

The Missionary Society enlisted other churches and clubs to join their effort. Before long, they established a community space in the factory district that included a kitchen, dining room, and a place for reading or resting. It was clean, bright, and cheerful. A committee of volunteers came every day to make a low-cost hot lunch for the factory girls who arrived.

All these projects benefited the working people and low-income residents of Evansville. But Albion couldn't stop thinking about their homes. As she saw it, terrible housing conditions

General Cigar Company

were the cause of many of the troubles charitable groups tried to address. No one would ever solve these problems without rooting out the source. Bacon studied the situation and came to the

> definite conviction that I could do more for child welfare and for civic [city] welfare, more to fight tuberculosis and typhoid, more to prevent vice [wickedness] . . . by bettering the homes of our city than by all the varied lines of effort that had engrossed [interested] me.[2]

She understood that people who lived in overcrowded spaces without clean air and water were far more likely to become ill than those in roomier homes with running water and access to fresh air. Illnesses were far more likely to spread from one family member to another and on to other families when people lived so close together. When eight or nine families shared one uncovered cistern (a tank for catching rainwater) as their only water source, parents couldn't keep their children clean or safe from disease. They couldn't wash clothing or bedding. They couldn't even make safe meals. Imagine how those people felt, knowing that other children had a much better chance in life than theirs did.

People who had absolutely no alone time or privacy—not even a private toilet—were more likely to lash out in anger. They were more likely to become depressed. The elderly who lived in dark, damp rooms were more likely to suffer from painful joints and skin sores. Small children with no place to play couldn't easily develop their social skills or creativity. And what about young people with no place to go and no way to avoid contact with shady characters and even criminals? They were more likely to get into trouble themselves.

Bacon decided that if landlords wouldn't listen to reason or calls for humane treatment of tenants, the only thing that could bring relief to the poor was a housing law. Evansville had a mayor and a city council—a municipal government. Didn't they see their responsibility in this? The government's responsibility to protect all its citizens? It was time they did.

In 1907, Bacon learned that the city was going to consider a building ordinance (a local law passed by a municipal government). She hoped that the council would include regulations for tenements in the ordinance. But she didn't trust that they would.

Albion had avoided the world of politics throughout her life. But now she went straight to the mayor and described her idea and the need for it.

Yes, he told her. He would support tenement regulations in the ordinance. But there was a catch. He went on, "You go home and prepare the proper sections."[3]

Albion herself should write the regulations? How? She wasn't a lawyer or a city planner. She'd never actually read an ordinance. But she was so happy to have the mayor's support, it didn't occur to her that she might not be able to do what he asked. Still, she would need examples. She raced home and immediately wrote letters to city governments in Chicago and New York and elsewhere—cities that had adopted tenement regulations in recent years.

When the thick, heavy packages arrived at her house, Bacon was dismayed. Whole books, thousands of pages of regulations, dealt with tiny details of issues she had never thought about and couldn't understand. Details like the proper distance between ceiling joists seemed to have nothing to do with making tenements more livable. At least not the tenements in Evansville.

Albion kept scanning page after page until she found what she was looking for. Requirements for "light and air, fire protection, water, drainage, sewerage, repairs, prevention of dampness,"[4] and more. It was now up to her to identify the regulations that made sense for Evansville and write them into a fairly short and simple document. Something city councilmen who, like her, knew nothing about construction could easily understand.

Hour after hour, day after day, Albion Bacon searched existing tenement laws and thought about how they might apply to Evansville. The work she'd done in her uncle's law firm all those years ago now paid off. She understood that every word of every regulation had to be clear and specific—like the description of ceiling joists was. How many square feet must an apartment be? How many windows? What size windows? Every regulation had to be reasonable, fair to landlords, and beneficial to the poor. Think about the work involved in such an enormous undertaking. Think about doing that work without formal training, and entirely alone.

Finally, finally the bill (a draft of a proposed law) was complete. But the council decided to postpone making its decision. They didn't explain why. They simply put the ordinance on hold. Indefinitely. Bacon could only sigh and wait. Months went by and nothing happened.

Was all that work for nothing? No, it wasn't for nothing, Albion told herself. Evansville wasn't the only place in Indiana with housing problems. A city ordinance would have been wonderful. But a state housing law would be even better. And Bacon was confident that she now knew how to go about it.

The State Conference of Charities held a meeting in Evansville in 1907 while Bacon's city ordinance remained on hold. Bacon was asked to write a paper on housing for the conference. When the time came, Albion Bacon presented her paper as a speech, although she hated the idea of speaking to a large audience. But she was determined to explain everything she had learned about the conditions in which so many Indianans lived. She called her paper "The Homes of the Poor." In addition to giving the speech, she talked to everyone she could at the conference and hosted a reception at her own home for conference attendees from all over Indiana.

Albion met politicians—all men—and directors of charities who supported her ideas. They agreed that a state law was the only way to make real progress. But several members of the conference told her the time was not "ripe."[5] Really? When *would* the time be ripe? How could anyone *not* be ready to improve the health and well-being of thousands of people?

Bacon had given her audience a huge number of facts in "The Homes of the Poor." But those facts hadn't convinced them to take serious action. They needed even more information.

Later she wrote:

> Surely, if we could furnish proof that the other cities of our state had slums, and could show their devastating effects, some organization . . . would attend to procuring [getting] the law.[6]

It would have to be an organization the men in the state legislature could not ignore. Women in all sorts of clubs and societies might be sympathetic to Albion's cause, but only men could vote to change things.

Bacon made a plan. She would gather details on conditions throughout the state—scientific data from every corner of Indiana. Once she had all the information, she would talk to experts who had achieved housing reform in other states. She would combine the various state laws herself, give the finished product to an organization that had influence with Indiana lawmakers, and hope for the best. "Somehow," Bacon said, "I never doubted that it could and would be done."[7]

CHAPTER 8

★★★

A Widening Sphere

Getting a housing law passed by the state legislature wasn't easy. Albion Bacon hadn't thought it would be. And in the end, it wasn't an organization with influence that got a housing law passed as she had planned. It was Albion's own "sheer, disinterested [unbiased] persistence."[1]

As part of her research, Bacon went to the 1908 National Charities Conference in Richmond, Virginia, to talk to experts on housing. She used the office skills she'd acquired years earlier to take notes. She sent away for books and documents. She wrote to the famous author, photographer, and reformer Jacob Riis. Riis suggested she contact Lawrence Veiller, who had written New York's Tenement House Act of 1901—the first serious law of its kind in the country.

Bacon and Riis continued to correspond and she treasured his letters, always filled with "cheer and encouragement." She kept those letters and wrote, "Our family has always understood that if the house should take fire they must save the twins first, and then those letters."[2]

Albion also spent countless hours at the law library in the courthouse to study any laws already enacted in Indiana.

Jacob Riis, around 1900

Imagine her shock when she learned that "the poor in our state had no legal right to light and air."[3] How could that be? Weren't those basic human needs?

Next, Bacon developed a questionnaire and sent it to every charity in the state, asking for details of housing conditions in their areas. They reported on dreadful company housing in mining towns. Immigrant mill workers sharing beds between day shift and night shift workers. As many as twenty men living in two windowless rooms. Most towns, she learned, did not provide running water or sewers in the poorest neighborhoods.

Albion knew that words, even powerful words, would not be enough to sway legislatures. So she asked the state charities to send photographs as well. She mounted them on posters with captions and her own illustrations, including a huge skeleton hovering over the photograph of a terrible shack. She added the words, "Death keeps watch over this house."[4] Bacon traveled to many of Indiana's smallest towns to find information herself. The work went on through the summer of 1908. As summer ended and fall began, Albion spent her days writing letters to clubs, civic organizations, charities, influential men and women—all while the twins "played about me or sat as close as possible while I wrote, with little arms about my waist."[5]

Bacon's husband Hilary supported Albion throughout these efforts. She received no income from her research or lobbying, so part of his salary went toward her travel expenses, office supplies, postage, and more. The Bacons could afford to hire a cook and maids to help with the household, but Albion refused to employ a secretary to do typing and filing, even though that would have saved her a lot of time. The problem was that having a secretary would create a scandal. Married women with children simply didn't do the kind of work Albion was doing. She didn't dare draw attention to how she spent her days. She just forged on, doing the best she could to complete the bill without abandoning her children altogether.

Albion worked while the older children were away from home and the twins were napping. She worked after they went to bed. She no longer read for pleasure or saw friends. She didn't take long walks or plan social events. Her art was a thing of the past. Albion Bacon's life had become her family and the bill—mostly the bill. She wrote that no one could look at her without thinking of slums, and joked, "I almost feel as if my name is Bill."[6]

Finally, after nearly a year of tireless work, the document was ready. Albion sent it to a lawyer to be sure she'd used correct legal language and then took the bill with her to South Bend, Indiana, where she was to speak at the State Conference of Charities in October 1908. There she received an invitation to present her bill to the Indianapolis Commercial Club (now the Chamber of Commerce), an organization of businessmen with a lot of influence in the state legislature.

Albion remembered being "rigid" with tension and too nervous to eat the lunch served at the meeting. She told herself to keep her words and tone businesslike and to avoid emotion. She knew she couldn't afford to appear too "womanly" in a room filled with businessmen. A room not intended for a petite woman like Albion Bacon. As she wrote later, "If anything makes it difficult to maintain a lofty dignity it is to sit in chairs built for great men, conscious that you can't reach the floor."[7]

Despite Bacon's misgivings, the club members liked the bill and said they would support it. That was exactly what Bacon had hoped for. These men could get the bill passed. Finally, Albion could go home and resume her old life.

No, the committee members said. "We will do all we can to push it, but you will have to be the leader."[8]

Albion felt like she might faint. She couldn't lead the way on this. She'd never even been to the state legislature, for heaven's sake. Besides, this assignment would require her to be in Indianapolis constantly, away from her children even more than she'd been this past year.

Bacon wrote later, "I saw myself with horror, a married woman with a 'career.'"[9] She imagined her unsupervised twins going out in the rain without boots and getting sick. She thought of her older daughters going out into society without their mother there to guide them. And what about her

Indiana state house

husband, who'd been so patient and supportive through all of this? Would he stand for her being involved in actual politics? Politics was harsh and ugly. It was no place for a woman, in Albion's mind. Especially a shy, timid woman.

Then Bacon pictured the children who didn't have boots, and teenage girls who didn't have even one nice dress. The women without supportive husbands or any husband at all. She went home and told her family what the Commercial Club had asked of her.

"Go!" they said. "We'll manage." Bacon felt petrified of what lay ahead. She feared that her family would bear the brunt of a public scandal over her work. She worried that she might not be up to the task and the bill would fail because of it. Still, Albion packed her bags. Her fear, she said, gave her "the same sensation that the Big Dog always gave me in childhood."[10] But her family's unwavering support gave her the courage to keep going.

Through most of January and February 1909, Albion Bacon lobbied, educated, persuaded, pushed, and pestered the men of Indiana's state legislature for a tenement bill. She soon found that "apathy" was a big obstacle—the men simply didn't care. So Bacon talked to legislators' wives, who tended to be sympathetic. She talked to the public. *Someone* had to care. She spent hours at the statehouse, where she hung her photograph posters in the hallway and talked about the bill with anyone who would listen. And she spoke to a joint meeting of the Indiana House and Senate health committees.

Albion decided to set aside her nonemotional, not-too-womanly tone as she faced a tired, distracted audience of lawmakers on the evening of January 19. She spoke from her heart. The next day, a reporter called her speech "eloquent" and commented on how impressed the committee members had been. But Albion knew that eloquence wasn't enough. She kept working.

Finally, in March 1909, a weakened version of Albion's bill passed. It applied only to the state's two biggest cities—Indianapolis and Evansville. Not surprisingly, the strongest opponents of the bill were members of the state senate who owned tenement buildings themselves. Imagine that level of greed (it still exists today). But Albion had done all she could. The new law was better than nothing, she said. Perhaps it would lead to a stronger bill in the future. She went home, intending never to come back to Indianapolis.[11]

RUSSELL SAGE
FOUNDATION

A MODEL
TENEMENT HOUSE
LAW

BY
LAWRENCE VEILLER
AUTHOR OF "HOUSING REFORM," ETC.

NEW YORK
CHARITIES PUBLICATION
COMMITTEE . . . . MCMX

A model tenement house law, written by Lawrence Veiller

Two years later, Bacon was back in the state capital. She couldn't help herself. As she had hoped, a new bill was under consideration, and she sensed that public support was increasing. She had awakened people to a situation that had grown only worse since she'd started her efforts. But she needed to do more.

This time, she worked with Lawrence Veiller on every word of every regulation. Page after page after page of minute detail about windows, doors, lighting, bathrooms, and on. The document was divided into ninety-nine sections that filled hundreds of pages. The work was tedious and tiring. But after discussion and debate, the bill passed eighty-two to two in the House. One newspaper referred to Mrs. Bacon's "indefatigable work."[12] Yet the battle wasn't over.

One member of the Senate—a man who owned some of the worst tenements in the entire country—pushed his colleagues to oppose the bill. It was defeated by one vote. Think of Bacon's frustration. She was exhausted and disappointed. Politics really was as ugly as she had feared years earlier. But this time, she had no intention of looking the other way or giving up.[13]

The "brave little woman," as one reporter called her, spoke to clubs and conferences all over the state.[14] She wrote articles for newspapers. And while she had never had time or interest for women's clubs, she found that those organizations had shifted their focus from culture to reforms, and she now embraced them. By 1913, Bacon had built a huge network of support from people of every economic background, including middle-class clubwomen and male politicians. Her efforts paid off. Indiana's Housing Act of 1913 passed with big majorities in both the House and Senate. The work was done.[15] Or was it? Soon after she got home, Albion told a reporter, "The [1913] housing bill is just the first step."[16]

Bacon knew that public opinion was moving in her direction and did everything she could to move it faster. She used photographs to push some people to consider the human and moral cost of doing nothing. For others, especially those who insisted that poverty was a person's own fault, she pointed out that the state's financial cost for enforcing housing laws was far, far less than the cost of supporting orphans and very young lawbreakers, men unable to work because of tuberculosis, and so much more. She had the research to back up her arguments.

Even after the defeat of a stronger law in 1915, Bacon didn't quit. By 1917, she had the votes to pass what newspapers called the Death Trap Bill. It would regulate more kinds of housing than the earlier law did. And it would give health authorities the same kind of power over dangerously unhealthy buildings that fire marshals had over firetraps—buildings filled with fire hazards.[17] It was an enormous victory. Albion deserved to rest. But she had more to do.

Bacon always thought of herself as belonging in the domestic sphere, even when she traveled and gave speeches and wrote papers. But she knew that once she took up the cause of housing, her sphere had changed shape. It didn't look exactly like most middle-class women's spheres anymore. Admittedly, she'd never been much of a cook. And fortunately, she could afford a lot of hired household help. Did that make her a failure as a wife and mother? That was how society judged women's success, after all. Albion was torn between her vision of domestic responsibility and her work. But as her youngest daughter said, "Anybody could do the [housework]. Not anybody could do what Mother was doing."[18]

Albion Bacon's sphere continued to widen even after she got the housing law passed. She worked to end child labor. She organized an enormous health research project for the Children's Bureau (the agency Lillian Wald had suggested to Theodore Roosevelt). She fought for expanded school attendance laws. She lobbied to improve Indiana's juvenile justice system so that young people who broke the law weren't thrown into prison with hardened criminals. She did all this and more.

Bacon didn't call herself a progressive, but that was exactly what she was. She saw her duty as maintaining the home, but like Lillian Wald, her idea of "home" had grown. It came to include the neighborhood, the school, and eventually the city and the entire state in which she lived. She had overcome her shy, timid ways to become "Indiana's Municipal Housekeeper."

And she wasn't the only progressive woman cleaning house.

CHAPTER 9

★★★

Stark Reality

Chicago was a city of opportunity for a child like Lugenia Burns in the 1880s. That was why her mother, Louisa, had moved the family there from St. Louis after her husband Ferdinand died when Lugenia was in elementary school. The Burnses' oldest daughter already lived in Chicago with her husband and children. She was a teacher and felt confident that her nearly grown brothers would be able to find good jobs there as she had. Moreover, Lugenia, the youngest of the seven Burns children, would be able to attend much better schools than she could in St. Louis. That was important. Anyone could see that young Lugenia Burns was very bright.

Lugenia made the most of her opportunities. She finished elementary school and did well in high school at a time when very few American children went beyond seventh or eighth grade. She then found work as a secretary and took classes at the Chicago School of Design and at the Chicago Art Institute.

As full as her life was as she entered adulthood, though, Lugenia was well aware of the restrictions she faced. And not only the restrictions faced by every young woman in the United States in the late 1800s. Of course she couldn't vote. She couldn't control her own property if she married. She couldn't go to most colleges. But in addition to those limits, Lugenia couldn't attend services at just any church. She couldn't join just any women's club. And she knew she wasn't welcome in most neighborhoods. As a young Black woman, Lugenia Burns experienced segregation and racism every day.

Race relations in Chicago were generally peaceful compared with many other parts of the country. Black men there voted and held office. But Chicago, the second-largest city in the country after New York in 1890, was segregated. Black Chicagoans lived in the "Black Belt" of the city. They organized their own clubs and churches and owned their own businesses. But they generally did not mix with white Chicagoans, and their economic opportunities were limited. Lugenia Burns knew it didn't have to be that way. She had proof.

Lugenia Burns Hope, 1908

When two of Lugenia's older brothers lost their jobs and the third got married during the early 1890s, Burns gave up her art classes and found ways to earn more money and help support the family. She worked as a bookkeeper and as a dressmaker. She then accepted a job as a secretary to the board of a local charity. Burns was the first Black person to hold that position and got along well with her white co-workers. Didn't that show that Black and white people could work together?

Lugenia then added a part-time job as an assistant to a local businesswoman to her schedule. Her new job opened the way for more interracial experience and reinforced Lugenia's certainty that progress could be made.[1]

One day Lugenia's part-time employer, Mrs. Warne, took her to Hull House, founded in 1890 as one of the first settlement houses in the country. She felt quite welcome there. Hull House's white founders, Jane Addams and Ellen Starr, did not believe in segregation. That was true at Lillian Wald's Henry Street Settlement, too, but those two settlement houses were exceptional in that way.

Lugenia continued to visit Hull House as Mrs. Warne's assistant every week. She admired the settlement's social work with the city's immigrant community—a mix of Irish, Italian, German, Russian, and Greek newcomers. They were Jews, Catholics, Orthodox Christians, and more. All were welcome at Hull House.

The settlement's social workers used a scientific approach in studying the community. They used their data to find solutions for the problems their community faced—from the need for job skills to hunger and language barriers. Lugenia watched and learned. And she got to know people of many different backgrounds. Most Chicagoans didn't have that kind of experience.

In 1893, at just twenty-two years old, Lugenia Burns was now her family's main source of income. She wished she could go back to her art classes, but she didn't complain. It felt good to be able to support herself and her family. And both of her jobs were rewarding. She liked being self-sufficient and she liked helping people.

What she didn't like was the pointless racism that oozed through most of the city and into the lives of all Black Chicagoans. The racism that seeped into the biggest event the city had ever hosted—the 1893 Columbian Exposition, also known as the Chicago World's Fair.

The exposition had two purposes. One was to celebrate the four hundredth anniversary of Columbus's arrival in the Americas (he arrived in 1492, but the fair's opening was delayed by several months). The other was to show the world America's accomplishments.

Large Ferris wheel at the World's Columbian Exposition, Chicago

Millionaire capitalists had financed much of the exposition. These were "new money" men such as meat tycoons Philip Armour and Gustavus Swift, inventor Cyrus McCormick, department store owner Marshall Field, and many others. They were proud of their achievements and eager to display the latest advances in agriculture, manufacturing, transportation, energy, new foods (including Cracker Jack and chewing gum), and much more—including the world's first Ferris wheel, named for the man who designed it for the fair.

States exhibited their economic and cultural strengths, as

did fifty foreign countries ranging from France and Germany to Japan, Columbia, Turkey, and East India.

More than one hundred thousand visitors streamed through the gates of the Chicago World's Fair on opening day—May 1, 1893. Imagine how crowded the streets must have been in a city of just over one million people. Before the exposition ended six months later, some twenty-seven million people—equal to nearly one half of the population of the United States—had been to the fair.[2]

Visitors admired the carefully chosen flowers and trees that filled the fairgrounds. They commented on the beautiful, elegant buildings lining a lovely man-made lake. Those buildings looked just like white marble and inspired the nickname for the exposition, "the White City."

Exposition grounds, World's Columbian Exposition, Chicago

Anyone who looked more closely at the fairgrounds and the fair, though, would have seen something else. The "marble" buildings were actually temporary structures made of plaster and painted white. They were beautiful, but misleading, a bit fake. So was the fair itself.

The public read about the financiers, architects,

and designers of the event. The famous, powerful men who had everyone's admiration. To most people, those men represented America's astonishing achievements. But visitors to the fair—and the millions who read about it in newspapers and magazines—saw nothing that acknowledged the forty thousand workers who built the hundreds of buildings and exhibits. Or the six thousand men who were injured in the process, or became ill in the fair's terrible working and living conditions. It didn't acknowledge the thirty workers who had died.[3]

The fair celebrated Christopher Columbus. But it made no mention of the dreadful consequences his arrival had for Indigenous peoples (most Americans didn't worry about or talk about that then). Fair officials set aside special days to celebrate immigrants from Germany, Poland, Ireland, and many other European countries. They set aside days to honor train workers, carriage makers, fishermen, and more.[4] But the fair's planning committees had excluded Black representatives, though there were far more Black Americans in the United States than there were Polish immigrants or carriage makers. State committees and fair organizers had rejected every proposal for exhibits on Black culture and achievements. It seemed "the White City" was an accurate nickname in more than one way.

After months of protest by Black leaders around the country, fair officials announced that August 25 would be "Colored Americans Day." It was also called "Negro Day" (both "colored" and "Negro" were accepted terms for Americans of African ancestry at the time, like saying "people of color"). Journalist Ida B. Wells and others saw the day as an insult. Black Americans had played a fundamental part in building the nation since the 1600s. They'd been agricultural workers, soldiers, inventors, engineers, carpenters, ironworkers, farmers, teachers, artists, and more. Why weren't they mentioned throughout the exhibits?

Those leaders called for Black Americans to "boycott" the fair—to refuse to go.

Other prominent Black Americans, including Frederick Douglass—born enslaved and now an advisor to presidents—disagreed. Yes, one day was too little. But it could be an opportunity to reach a national and international audience. Douglass planned to give a speech at the fair on August 25.

A few days before the event, a local Black social club hosted a dance for Black visitors in town for the fair as well as Black Chicagoans. Lugenia Burns decided to attend with friends. Burns had a pleasant, intelligent face and a confident look. A skilled dressmaker, she knew how to dress very well and was a good conversationalist. A lot of young men found her very attractive, and she enjoyed their attention. But Lugenia valued her independence and wasn't interested in marriage. She had no desire to give up her work to cook and clean for a husband. She didn't want to ask anyone's permission to do things either. Lugenia Burns was quite content on her own. However, she met someone at the dance who made her think again.

John Hope was a student at Brown University in Rhode Island. He seemed a bit different from most of the young men Burns had met in Chicago. By the time the dance ended, Burns had

THE REASON WHY

The Colored American is not in the World's Columbian Exposition.

The Afro-American's Contribution to Columbian Literature

Copies sent to any address on receipt of three cents for postage. Address Miss Ida B. Wells, 128 S. Clark Street, Chicago, Ill., U. S. A.

World's Fair pamphlet

agreed to go with Hope to the World's Fair. She didn't find the young man particularly handsome, but something about the way he looked at her made her uneasy—in good way.

Hope was smitten. He and Lugenia spent the last few weeks of the summer going on picnics together. Then John went back to school. But he didn't plan to let go of Lugenia. He wrote to her and she wrote back. Slowly, the length and frequency of their letters increased.

John also found ways to return to Chicago. He graduated from Brown in 1894 and became a classics (Greek and Latin) instructor at a Black university in Nashville, Tennessee. But he took courses at the University of Chicago during the next three summers.

While in Chicago, Hope proposed to Lugenia. She turned him down. He proposed again. She turned him down again. How could she leave her aging mother or her life in Chicago for Tennessee? Besides, some of those other fellows she knew had proposed too. And Hope didn't seem to understand that Lugenia would never give up her work. Yet despite these concerns, Lugenia loved John and admired him.

John Hope was a "race man"—he believed in working for true equality for all Black Americans. He was serious about his studies. And while he didn't have money, he did have integrity and purpose. Those qualities were more important to

Morehouse College president John Hope and his wife, Lugenia, 1917

Lugenia than wealth. So, at last, four years after they met, Lugenia Burns and John Hope married in late 1897.[5]

Soon after, John accepted a teaching position at Atlanta Baptist College (later renamed Morehouse College), a Black men's school in Georgia. Atlanta was at the heart of the Deep South and perhaps the most segregated city in America in the late 1800s. Lugenia's mother was frightened for her daughter. She had good reason to feel that way.

In the years just after the Civil War, Black Americans had embraced their new freedom. The Fourteenth and Fifteenth Amendments had guaranteed Black Americans the same rights of citizenship that white Americans had. Black men voted and were elected to Congress and other offices. Black children went to school. But true freedom didn't last. Many white Southerners who couldn't adjust to the idea of Black and white people being equal fought back. They wanted to regain their supremacy, and their economic and political power.

By the late 1880s, the country backslid. Black men in the South could no longer vote or hold office. Southern states had found ways around the Fifteenth Amendment. Black Americans who had succeeded economically now faced restrictions on their businesses, on where they could live, and more. White lawmakers, including men who saw themselves as progressive, passed segregation bills known as Jim Crow laws. They believed that white supremacy was the natural order of the world. And some were quite willing to use violence to maintain white power.

Lugenia and John were well aware that Atlanta was particularly segregated. John had grown up in Georgia. They knew that racism, discrimination, and violence were on the rise there as they were in other places. But the couple planned to live in the main building on the college's small campus, where they'd be surrounded by students and other faculty. Surely, they thought, that would be safe.

On their first night in the tiny apartment on the second floor of the big brick Graves Hall, Lugenia heard shouting outside. It sounded like a fight of some sort, not far away. Then she heard gunfire. She didn't feel at all safe as the brawl, or whatever it was, went on throughout the night.[6] What had she been thinking? What had John been thinking? What kind of place had they come to? She soon learned what kind of place Atlanta was.

The city's Black population had grown from two thousand in 1860 to thirty-six thousand in 1900. But the areas where Black people could live did not expand. And Atlanta's municipal government made no improvements and provided no services for the overcrowded Black neighborhoods.[7] Atlanta Baptist College stood in the middle of one of those neighborhoods. So did nearby Spelman College, a Black women's school, and Atlanta University, another Black institution. All three had been established in the years just after the Civil War. Each had its own campus, but between and around them were unpaved and trash-filled streets, falling-down houses, and no running water. Children played in the smelly alleys within feet of drunks, thieves, and worse—a lot like what Albion Bacon had seen in Evansville, Indiana.

Lugenia soon got involved in efforts to improve the conditions in those neighborhoods. She and John had met a professor from Atlanta University—W. E. B. Du Bois—and they quickly became friends. Du Bois was very familiar with Chicago's Hull House, where Lugenia had volunteered and learned about social work. He'd corresponded with Jane Addams while he was involved in an enormous social research project and the resulting book, *The Philadelphia Negro*.[8] Impressed with Lugenia's

Graves (?) Hall, Atlanta Baptist College (now Morehouse)

knowledge of social work, he asked her to attend an upcoming local conference on "The Welfare of the Negro Child."

There, Lugenia met a group of middle-class Black women, many of them the wives of professors or business owners. They hoped to set up a free kindergarten for the children of neighboring workingwomen. Often, those women had no choice but to leave their preschool children locked in their homes alone all day (this is illegal today but sometimes still happens). A kindergarten would give those youngsters a half day of care, education, and a decent meal. Would Lugenia be willing to help raise money for this project? Of course. Would she lead the fundraising committee? Yes. It was exactly the kind of thing she'd been thinking about. And it was a way to continue her career.

The group's goal was to open one kindergarten in the fall of 1899. Lugenia and her committee raised enough money to open *two* kindergartens that year. They opened two more the next year, thanks to a local businessman. Alonzo Herndon had been born into slavery and was now the owner of barbershops,

John Hope *(back row, second from right)* and Alonzo Herndon *(back row, second from left)*

the founder of an insurance company, and one of the very few Black millionaires in the US. Herndon donated money to Lugenia's group. He also bought a building for the organization to use as a school and playground—the first playground for Black children in the area.[9]

It was a wonderful start. But after Lugenia and John's first child was born, Lugenia realized how very little there was for children to do in the neighborhood despite everyone's efforts. That had to change. She worked even harder, raising money and support to expand Black children's opportunities in Atlanta. Then, two events pushed her in a new direction.

CHAPTER 10

★★★

Community Organizing

Lugenia Hope knew about white supremacy, of course. Every Black American did. But she'd been protected from the worst of it during her years in Chicago. That protection disappeared on a warm Saturday night in September 1906.

For quite some time, Atlanta's newspapers had been promoting false or extremely exaggerated stories about the dangers white women faced from Black men. Why? Scandalous (for the time) headlines like "Bold Negro Kisses Girl's Hand" sold papers and made money for the publishers. So what if the stories weren't true?[1]

White men who chose to believe those stories (or at least use them as an excuse) often took matters into their own hands. Lynchings—or unauthorized public executions—increased to an average of one every month as angry white men went outside the law to horrifically murder Black men for the vaguest of "crimes." Without an arrest, without a trial, without evidence. But even that wasn't enough.

On that Saturday night in September 1906, tempers flared when more false stories appeared in papers and spread through rumors. In response, white men and some women formed mobs. It seemed they wanted to exterminate Black Americans altogether.

Years later, Lugenia wrote:

> When the storm broke it was Sat. night when Negroes were doing their marketing for Sun. They were at the market with their whole family. Out of a clear sky the white people began kicking—beating. They would stop the street cars, pull the Negroes out to beat them . . . This [kept] up until midnight.[2]

The violence spread throughout the city and continued on Sunday. John Hope, now the first Black president of Atlanta Baptist College, walked around the campus boundary. He had borrowed a gun for protection, and a faculty member joined him. But would they be able to stop a mob of angry people if they entered the grounds? The white leaders of the violent attacks had threatened to burn down all three Black colleges. Would they? Hope could see smoke and hear shouting, but news was hard to get.

Imagine everyone's fear that night. This was long before cell phones or televisions or radio. Most Black Atlantans didn't even have a telephone to spread or receive news and warnings of danger. Lugenia waited with others who lived on campus, not knowing whether her husband would live through the night. Not knowing how she would keep her small son safe if the mob came through the gates. There was nowhere to go.

Eventually, city leaders asked for state militia from other cities to come guard the Black colleges. Crowds of Black women and children flooded onto the campuses for safety. On Monday, the riots finally ended. The violence left Black residents terrorized and angry. It left Black businesses damaged or destroyed. At least twenty-five Black Atlantans had died at the hands of the mob.[3] The rest, including Lugenia and John Hope, had no choice but to go on with their lives as best they could.

Lugenia went on with her life by juggling a thousand things at once. As the wife of a college president, she hosted important guests, oversaw events, acted as a mother to homesick students, met with college donors, and more. She taught art and sewing classes. And she had a young child to care for. But she still felt responsible for the people in the neighborhood around the school and continued the work she'd started there. Every day seemed busier than the one before. But Hope still thought about what could be done to lift Atlanta's Black community beyond what a few kindergartens offered. Eventually, a neighborhood tragedy focused her ideas.

A young mother of three children had become ill. She was new to the community and too shy to reach out to her neighbors. The woman's husband and father didn't understand how sick she was, and they couldn't afford to stay home from work. After several days, a woman who lived nearby realized that she hadn't seen the young mother outside in a while. She decided to check on her. It was too late. The woman was terribly ill and died just hours later.

Lugenia felt the tragedy of the situation just as other women at and around the college did. This shouldn't have happened. Why had this woman been so isolated? Why hadn't her husband asked for help? Why hadn't anyone noticed sooner that something was wrong? They might have been able to save those three little children from losing their mother.

Hope thought back to her Chicago years and an idea gelled.

This was her chance to turn her thoughts into action. To take on something bigger than she had ever considered before. Between the terrible riots and the young woman's death, Lugenia Burns Hope had awakened to a clear vision of what she had to do.

"We have to work to get people together who have nothing in common and then get them sufficiently acquainted with each other to be able to work together," Lugenia Hope said.[4]

What did that mean? Hope knew that no one person or organization could solve the problems that had led to that young woman's death. All kinds of people had to work with one another to make real change—wealthy, poor, neighbors, experts, government, Black, and white. Bringing the various groups together would be an enormous job. Convincing them that they could work as one would be even harder. But Hope believed it could be done, despite the obstacles that Black reformers would have to overcome.

First, there were the issues of poverty. These were the same issues faced by immigrants and factory workers and others in American cities. Issues that Lillian Wald addressed by reforming health care in New York. That Albion Bacon tackled with housing reform in Indiana. That the women of Hull House dealt with in Chicago as they helped immigrants adapt to life in America.

But Black Americans faced a second set of issues that white Americans didn't. Issues caused and made worse by racism. Racism led city officials to deny Black residents basic services like clean water and schools even when they provided those services for white residents. Racism led politicians and publishers to frighten and enrage white people by promoting terrible stereotypes. It was an easy if dishonest way to get votes or sell papers (it still happens today with some politicians and some news outlets).

White men in power lied when they insisted that Black men were naturally violent, Black women had no morals, and Black children were less intelligent than white children. Those were hateful and ridiculous claims, but many white men and women were willing or even eager to believe what they heard and read. If one Black person broke the law, those white people assumed that all Black people broke the law. That was what the politicians said. It was what the newspapers said. The fact that no one could show any evidence to back up their claims didn't matter.

That kind of racism and fearmongering led white citizens to vote for racist candidates. It led politicians to pass laws that discriminated against Black Americans. It led to the violence of lynchings, and to the 1906 riots against Atlanta's Black communities.

That kind of racism hurt middle-class Black Americans as much as it hurt their lower-income neighbors. They could afford nice houses but weren't allowed to buy them. They could learn medicine or accounting or the law, but they couldn't serve white clients or get well-paying jobs. It went on and on and on.

Many Black reformers concluded that the only way to solve problems in Black communities was to defeat racism. But racism was and is based on fear and lies. Often, it is promoted by some of the wealthiest and most powerful people in society. How could *anyone* defeat that?

Lugenia Hope and other middle-class Black women believed they could defeat the fear and lies by showing white Americans that Black stereotypes were false. They could begin by being individual, visible examples of dignity, morality, and intelligence. That might create openings to do more. They also believed that as they worked toward success and acceptance in society for themselves, they had a duty to lift up their less fortunate neighbors with them for everyone's benefit.

✣✣✣

Hope invited a group of eight or nine women to discuss her ideas. Most of them were middle-class and prominent at the colleges and in the Black community. They supported Lugenia's plan. In 1908, the women organized a Neighborhood Union and elected Lugenia Burns Hope president. Their goal wasn't political. It was "the moral, social, intellectual, and religious uplift of the community and neighborhood."[5] The women hoped to make their corner of Atlanta a good place to raise children and combat racism at the same time.[6]

Lugenia Burns Hope and Neighborhood Union Group, around 1920

Children were key to Lugenia's vision. The birth of her second son made that focus even stronger. Hope still believed in a woman's domestic sphere, despite being active outside her family's home. But like Albion Bacon and other reformers, Lugenia's view of that sphere and of home was wide.

Hope family, early 1900s

"The home is the basis of a people's development," Hope believed. "A people" meant a community of people who shared a culture or history, not just one family. She believed that women, as mothers and moral models, were responsible for that development.[7] Not just in their own homes, but in their communities. The women of the Neighborhood Union agreed.

Under Hope's leadership, the Union zeroed in on a target area—West Fair, the neighborhood around the Atlanta Baptist campus.

They divided the area into districts and then divided the districts into sections.

The first step was to collect information on the families who lived there. Like Albion Bacon, Lugenia insisted that the Union contact every household in person. The Neighborhood Union needed accurate information—data—to figure out which issues were most critical. Hope enlisted students from Atlanta Baptist College and from Spelman College to help with the survey. The students were very useful to the Neighborhood Union. But the young people also benefited from their introduction to social work as part of their education. They soon interviewed a hundred families.

Once the questions and answers were sorted and recorded, Hope began to analyze the information. Of course, the data showed enormous need in the districts. No one was surprised. But the surveys narrowed that need into specific issues in distinct places.

Sewers, safer and cleaner water sources, and garbage collection would improve health throughout the community. Families with older children knew that recreation centers and more and better schools, especially a high school, would cut down on juvenile crime. People who lived on streets where bars and seedy hotels attracted problematic men and women wanted them gone. The needs of older people differed from the needs of their young neighbors in some ways. Mothers with babies had different wants from mothers with nearly grown children. The Union couldn't do everything at once. Who would it assist first? Children, they decided. The future.

The women agreed that the Union would do as much as it could for the children of the area until the local or state government took over meeting those essentials.[8] They argued that government held the real responsibility for many of the issues that made life difficult for so many people. Getting government to act on that responsibility was a high priority.

Like Lillian Wald, Albion Bacon, and Lugenia Hope, many progressive reformers had come to see charitable volunteer work as a temporary solution to city problems. After all, volunteers couldn't provide "infrastructure"—sewers, streetlights, paved roads, etc. Only government could do that. Only government could pass building codes or make education mandatory and finance schools.

All those public services cost money, of course. And government money comes from taxes collected from citizens. But citizens disagreed on how their tax money should be spent. Many wealthier people did not want to pay taxes to provide services for the poor, who they assumed didn't work as hard. Many native-born Americans didn't want to pay taxes to help immigrants get started. They would rather the country shut its doors. Many white people didn't want to pay for services in Black neighborhoods. And many Black citizens didn't think that working with white citizens could succeed. They didn't trust white people at all. Lugenia didn't give up. She believed that people should set aside their biases and bitterness and look out for the good of the entire community—not just their little piece of it.

Over the next several years, the Neighborhood Union continued to work in West Fair. It also expanded into other Black neighborhoods in Atlanta. By 1914, the Union had divided all of Atlanta's Black neighborhoods into zones. Every zone had districts and sections of districts. In each district, residents elected a president.

The result was that those residents didn't simply receive help from the Neighborhood Union. They were an active part of the organization. Think about that. Residents had a say in what the

Union did. They had a reason to pay attention to what was happening. They had "agency"—the power to *act* to better their lives instead of waiting for someone else to help them. And together, they might be able to make their voices heard.

For the next twenty-five years, Lugenia Hope led Atlanta's Neighborhood Union. She oversaw settlement houses in each zone. Departments under her leadership brought in speakers, acquired books for settlement libraries, and offered art and music classes, job-training classes, nursing, infant care, and more.

Members gathered signatures on petitions to remove "undesirable" residents from neighborhoods. But what did "undesirable" mean? Unfortunately, that depended on how members defined it based on their own values, expectations, and prejudices. Other petitions to the city government demanded better health care facilities. In the meantime, the Union recruited volunteer nurses and doctors, who made home visits. Eventually, the Neighborhood Union opened a health center.

Members also lobbied the city council to hire Black police officers. They petitioned for street improvements and streetlights, for health care and schools. And they pushed for voter registration. If politicians had to answer to more Black voters, the petitions and all other efforts would be far more effective.

Through it all, Atlanta's wall of racism remained an enormous obstacle. The city did not improve many streets or hire any Black officers. For years, there was no high school for Black students, and the schools that did exist were horribly overcrowded and in terrible shape. Instead of accepting responsibility for health care facilities and other services, the city handed the responsibility to the Neighborhood Union.[9] Meanwhile, new discriminatory laws made voting ever more difficult for Black citizens.

How did Hope and the other women keep moving forward in the face of such opposition? Like other progressive women,

Lugenia never considered quitting an option. Even the tiniest step forward was proof that progress was possible. And so, she persisted.

After the women of the Union had collected detailed information on the terrible conditions in the city's Black schools, Hope invited prominent white women to visit those schools. She wanted them to witness the reality of the city's policies in the lives of Black children. Those who accepted the invitation were shocked at what they saw. Some felt moved to support change.

The city still made only very small improvements. But the fact that at least some white women had worked with the Black community was hopeful (Atlanta opened a high school for Black teens in 1924).[10] Lugenia worked to build on this momentum.

When the Atlanta Anti-Tuberculosis Association called for a meeting including both white and Black groups, Hope was ready. She pointed out to white women that segregated neighborhoods and schools meant nothing to a contagious disease. Black and white Atlantans came in contact with one another anyway. Stopping tuberculosis had to be an integrated project. Plans to slow the spread of the illness throughout the city went forward. And the Anti-Tuberculosis Association used Lugenia's Neighborhood Union organizational system to collect data.

Hope went on to challenge the Young Women's Christian Association (YWCA) to open a branch for young Black women in Atlanta. Having accomplished that, she then fought discrimination in the YWCA's leadership. All the while, she headed the Neighborhood Union as it continued to offer health education and health care, job training, childcare, playgrounds, and more.

While Lugenia Burns Hope pressed for improved city services, better health care, and better schools for Black Americans in

Atlanta through community organizing, progressive women in the North organized in a different way. They worked to improve the lives of thousands of workingwomen in factories, mills, and shops. Like Hope and her allies, they too faced enormous obstacles.

CHAPTER 11

"I Know Whereof I Speak"

Leonora O'Reilly stood tall, straight, and confident whether she was on a street corner talking to a dozen garment workers or at a podium in front of an audience of thousands. Her "rich and sympathetic and stirring" voice had a way of quieting a room and drawing everyone's attention.[1] O'Reilly always sounded sure of herself. Even when she knew that most of her audience disagreed with just about everything she said.

Like other women labor leaders and suffragists, Leonora O'Reilly had faced plenty of opposition over the years. O'Reilly and other women had been called unfeminine and unladylike for speaking in public and being paid for it. And making demands for factory girls, mill girls, and shopgirls? How dare they?

Leonora had heard that criticism and far worse. She ignored it. The public needed to hear what she had to say. She accepted money for speaking so that she could put food on the table. As for being "unladylike," Leonora O'Reilly wasn't part of Mrs. Astor's society and didn't care to be. And she didn't call herself or her co-workers "factory girls." Or mill girls or shopgirls. They weren't girls. They were women. Workingwomen. They had as much right to speak up for themselves, to demand dignity and respect, as any American. How dare anyone think otherwise?

Leonora O'Reilly was a progressive and a reformer. But her path to the progressive movement was different from the paths of women like Lillian Wald, Albion Bacon, and Lugenia Hope. O'Reilly didn't have an awakening moment. She didn't suddenly come upon the reality of life for poor Americans the way so many middle-class women did. Leonora didn't need an awakening. She'd been part of the working poor for most of her life. She'd lived the reality. As she said, "I . . . know whereof I speak."[2]

Pencil drawing of Leonora O'Reilly, 1912

Leonora's mother, Winifred, had come to the United States as a young girl. Winifred and her parents were among the hundreds of thousands of Irish immigrants who had fled the terrible famine sweeping through Ireland in the late 1840s. Eventually, Winifred followed her own mother and took a job in the garment (clothing) industry in New York City. Leonora's father, John O'Reilly, was also an Irish immigrant and a printer. Together, he and Winifred managed to make ends meet and had high hopes for their baby girl. But Leonora was just a year old when John O'Reilly died in 1871. From that moment, everything changed.

In those days, very few people had life insurance, and

government did not provide any "safety nets." No financial help to widows and their children. No Social Security for children without fathers. No Medicaid to help the poor with health expenses. No food assistance programs. No unemployment insurance or help for workers injured on the job.

Leonora's mother faced a terrible future. If she went back to work in a garment factory to support herself and her child, it would mean a ten-hour day away from home. She'd have to leave her daughter with neighbors if she was lucky enough to have neighbors willing to look after a baby. If she took work into her home instead—sewing or doing laundry—she wouldn't make enough money to pay her rent. Leonora might be taken away from her. Winifred O'Reilly had seen that happen to other widows. In fact, the majority of children in New York's orphanages—children like Rose Schneiderman and her siblings—weren't orphans at all. They had at least one living parent, but that parent couldn't support them.

There was no choice. Winifred O'Reilly took a factory job. She also did sewing work at home in the evenings and rented space to boarders to earn a little more money. But no matter how hard she worked, or how many hours she put in, it wasn't enough.

Winifred knew that little Leonora was a very intelligent child. She dreamed of her daughter finishing school and making a bright future for herself. But that dream was out of reach for a working-class widow's child. At the age of thirteen, Leonora left school to take a job in a factory that made collars for men's shirts (men's dress shirts in the late 1800s had removable collars).

Leonora wasn't a bit unusual in quitting school at that age. Thousands of children in New York and elsewhere did the same. Some left school much earlier. Imagine heading off each morning to spend ten or even twelve hours in a factory before completing the sixth grade. Imagine breathing in fabric dust and lint all day, every day. No more school. No more recess or playtime. No more afternoons in the sunshine and fresh air.

Leonora had loved school. But she didn't complain. She knew she was one of the lucky ones. With her wages added to her mother's income, no one would take her away. She and her mother would stay together. They'd have enough to eat. At least most of the time.

Winifred didn't give up her dream of a better life for her daughter. She and Leonora spent their evenings educating themselves. One read aloud as the other did the dishes or worked on sewing jobs. They read books on history, economics, sociology, and philosophy. They went to lectures and classes at Cooper Union, a free school that provided evening courses in sciences, literature, art, and more for anyone who wanted to learn. Cooper Union also offered lectures by experts in political science, psychology, and many other topics.[3] Leonora was like a sponge, soaking up facts and ideas and remembering just about everything.

By the time O'Reilly was sixteen, she had moved to a job in a factory that made "shirtwaists"—women's blouses worn with a long skirt. Twenty or so women spent all day hunched over their sewing machines in one crowded room. The work was repetitive and tedious, but it was a bit better than the collar factory. Leonora knew that the low pay, long hours, and lack of breaks weren't fair. She felt the same fatigue the other workers felt after seven or eight hours. But they all still had two or three hours left to go each day.

O'Reilly realized that most accidents in that factory and others happened late in the day, when workers were practically asleep at their machines. She didn't want to accidentally run the machine's needle through her hand as some exhausted women

Shirtwaist, around 1900

had done. She didn't want to catch her clothing or her hair in the wheels. And everyone was afraid of fire in the wood-floored room filled with wooden tables and yards upon yards of flammable fabric. The women in those buildings just wanted to get through those last hours of work safely. And that kind of factory wasn't nearly as dangerous as some.

Years later, Leonora described the "sinking, all-gone feeling" workers had at the end of a ten-hour day. They didn't have "energy enough to even jump over a puddle" as they dragged themselves home, she said.[4] Surely, there must be a better way.

O'Reilly's godfather, a French immigrant, belonged to the Knights of Labor—an organization of workers from various trades. She asked him about the Knights and whether she could join. Few labor organizations at the time admitted women, but the Knights did. Leonora and her mother both joined. But they saw right away that the handful of women at the meetings stayed quiet. None held a leadership position.[5] That would not work for Leonora O'Reilly.

She and some of the other young women she'd met at the meetings soon set up their own organization—the Working Women's Society (WWS) in 1886. They agreed that using *women* rather than *girls* in the title was an important step toward gaining respect and equality. Moreover, the society was not a social club, as many workingwomen's groups were. Members weren't interested in cooking classes or lessons in childcare. No. The WWS was a labor union. These workingwomen were fighting for an eight-hour workday, fair wages, and safe conditions. Just like working men. Like the railroad workers, miners, steelworkers, and others across the country who had organized during the last several years.

No one person could convince a business owner to pay more or make a workplace safe or protect a worker who was injured. But organized groups of workers—unions—could have some power. Couldn't they?

Business owners and industrial tycoons refused to acknowledge the unions. They tried to stop workers from organizing and

State militia entering Homestead, Pennsylvania

from striking. Owners "blacklisted" anyone who joined a union—making sure that worker would not be able to get a job anywhere. They also hired armed security forces who didn't hesitate to use violence against the workers. Police often used violence too.

In July 1892, seven steelworkers at one of Andrew Carnegie's biggest Pennsylvania steel mills were killed in a gun battle between striking workers and security forces. Three security men also died. The governor called in the state militia (today's National Guard), but the strike and the violence went on for four months. In the end, the strikers were defeated. They went back to work and Carnegie slashed their wages. The same kind of thing happened at mills and mines nationwide.

Some union leaders believed that workers would never get fair treatment from business owners. Certainly not while those owners used their money to control state governments and the police and other positions of power. They argued that the existing economic system no longer worked in the new industrial world. "Capitalism"—private ownership of resources, land, and production—had to change. Workers needed a new system. A system in which the people who actually did the work owned and ran the businesses.

Other labor leaders agreed that private owners and corporations had only one goal—making money. If allowed, they would always treat workers like machines. These leaders called for the government to take over the nation's biggest industries, as well as banks and railroads.

Those were revolutionary ideas and frightened most Americans. But while the majority of workers wanted change, they didn't want revolution. They didn't want a civil war between workers and industrialists. O'Reilly, too, was against violent revolution. Deep down, she hoped that someday people could live together without any government. But she knew that wasn't realistic in her own time. And she agreed with many other labor leaders that workers could eventually make progress within the existing system if they all stuck together.

Business owners were already against labor organizations, whether those organizations called for revolution or not. To the owners, any labor organization was bad. The idea of a labor organization for women was even worse. After all, workingwomen were . . . well . . . women. In business owners' eyes, women didn't belong in the rough-and-tumble world of economics or politics. For one thing, they were too delicate. For another, they belonged at home. And if some women did take jobs, they certainly didn't deserve the same wages as men. Women, the industrialists argued, didn't have the skills men did. Besides, they weren't breadwinners. They weren't the ones providing for families. Men were. Women didn't need the money. Men did.

Leonora scoffed at those ideas. Her own mother was living proof that women were *not* delicate. No one working in a factory of any kind could afford to be delicate. And women *did* have skills. Excellent skills. They *were* breadwinners. They *were* supporting families. And they *did* need money. More money than wealthy industrialists were willing to pay them.

It wasn't just business owners that organizers like O'Reilly were up against. Many middle-class Americans opposed unions too. They were afraid of strikes that could lead to shortages of items they needed or wanted. They were afraid that violence between workers and security forces might spread into the streets of their own towns and cities. They were afraid of the radical ideas that some union leaders supported, of a shift to communism or socialism (though few people could have said exactly what communism and socialism *were*). Fear of what might happen to their own way of life was one reason some middle-class men and women supported reform. They hoped to keep workers from supporting radical ideas or violence.

As for women organizing, that presented something else to fear. If women in factories and mills organized, what then? Would the working-class women who the middle class employed in their homes join unions? A lot of well-off Americans, even reformers, didn't want their own maids or cooks or laundresses demanding more pay or shorter hours.

How could the Working Women's Society win support with all that opposition?

Leonora O'Reilly had a natural ability to connect with all sorts of people. She faced criticism for speaking in public and for what she said. But most people who heard her speak or met her one-on-one came away liking her.

O'Reilly didn't think she was above other factory workers because she was well-read and well-spoken. She didn't think she was below educated people because she'd left school so young. When she met a reformer who had studied in Germany and published poetry and essays, she amazed the woman with her "astounding familiarity with the great writers, both of history and economics."[6] Talking about history and economics was second nature to Leonora. So was talking about her own experience as a working woman.

O'Reilly used her people skills to gain support for the WWS. She organized meetings and invited department store workers to come and talk about their jobs openly. From the outside, work as a "shopgirl" looked like a good way to earn a living. Stores were clean. There were no dangerous machines. And the girls always dressed well and had lovely manners. But that was not the whole story.

Leonora knew these young women needed help. She invited Josephine Shaw Lowell, the head of the New York State Board of Charities, to come listen to them. Lowell had never been a shopgirl. She'd never needed a job of any kind. She was part of a prominent and wealthy Massachusetts family (her brother Robert Gould Shaw had been killed leading the famous 54th Massachusetts Regiment of Black soldiers during the Civil War). The white abolitionist Shaw family had a long history of working for many kinds of reform, and Josephine was no exception. Now in her forties, she'd been involved in charitable work for many years. She didn't have the right to vote, of course, but she did have influence in New York politics. And Leonora had had her support since the early days of the WWS.

Lowell accepted O'Reilly's invitation. She listened as the young shop women described their long hours and demanding responsibilities. They had to dress well, but they had to buy those clothes out of their pathetically low wages. They were on their feet hour after hour with no breaks. Worse, the women frequently faced sexual harassment. No matter what store they worked for, even the finest places selling high-quality goods, shopgirls could expect exploitation and abuse from their bosses.

As Leonora had hoped, Josephine Shaw Lowell wanted to help. Listening to those young women was an awakening for her. She volunteered to oversee a thorough study of department store employees. Alice Woodbridge, a former shopgirl, led a team that interviewed many women working in retail. Lowell then organized a report and made the results public so that customers—mostly women—would know what was happening to the young ladies who helped them with their shopping.

Next, Lowell helped form the Consumers' League of New York in 1891. Workers' groups sometimes asked the public to boycott (refuse to buy from) businesses that were particularly awful to their workers. That practice wasn't new. But the Consumers' League took a different approach. They made a list of stores that treated employees well and encouraged shoppers—"consumers"—to buy from those stores. The league didn't punish store owners for being bad employers. It rewarded those who were good employers. And women who shopped at the approved stores felt like they were contributing to a cause without having to give up the products they wanted to buy.

The list of recommended stores was terribly short at first. But it grew over time as more businesses improved their practices. Store owners wanted to be on that list. They couldn't be sure that a place on the list would bring in new customers, but it seemed worth trying.

The league also identified products made by responsible manufacturers. Many middle-class women were happy to buy those goods. Often, it wasn't because they cared about working-women. It was because the league pointed out that those goods were clean and safe. No one coughing with tuberculosis had sewn the garment. No unskilled child had used the fabric to wipe away sweat or snot. But whatever the consumers' motivation was, their support helped factory workers. Unfortunately, it had a negative impact on women who produced goods in their own homes, since they had no way to meet league standards.[7] But helping factory workers was a step forward. And progress is never smooth.

Similar leagues formed in other cities. They came together as the National Consumers League in 1899. The NCL still exists today.

O'Reilly, not yet twenty years old when they met, appreciated Lowell's experience and expertise. She cheered the woman's efforts to improve the lot of shopgirls. She was glad to have the support of other wealthy and middle-class women too. But Leonora disagreed with them on some things.

Many middle-class and upper-class reformers thought that women should make their demands gently. Lowell suggested that women should be careful not to "scold" employers. They should be aware of how the public might react to loud speeches, marches, and demonstrations. She argued that women workers might put themselves in a negative light.[8]

Leonora rejected the "ladylike" approach. She encouraged workingwomen to *demand* the same pay men got for the same jobs. To *demand* the same rights men had. Not ask gently. And she criticized "some of the best-intentioned people in the world" for viewing men's and women's demands for better wages differently. For supporting men who spoke up or went out on strike while discouraging women from doing the same thing "through fear that workingwomen may do something 'unladylike.'"[9]

O'Reilly flatly refused to soften her speeches or take a gentle approach. After all, there was nothing gentle in the work women like her did. The middle- and upper-class women in the WWS cringed at how forcefully O'Reilly spoke. But they continued to support her.[10] As one person said, Leonora was "so intense that few dared contradict her."[11] And most of the women admired her even while they shook their heads at her public speeches. However, some of her supporters worried about her. They thought she was working so hard that she might ruin her health or worse.

CHAPTER 12

★★★

Agitating

Leonora O'Reilly, with her fair skin, soft dark hair, and ready smile, was often described as beautiful. But she was also very thin, sometimes pale rather than fair, and she rarely rested. She still worked full-time as a forewoman at a shirtwaist factory even while she promoted the WWS. And she hadn't given up reading serious academic books and taking business classes at night. Where did she find the energy to do all that and still prepare and deliver such fiery speeches? It seemed impossible to keep up such a pace. When would it all catch up with her?

Louise Perkins was one of the women who supported the WWS and admired Leonora O'Reilly. Perkins was wealthy, but like Josephine Shaw Lowell, she chose to use her time and talent to benefit others and worked as a teacher. She and Leonora had become friends in New York and stayed in touch through letters when Perkins moved to Massachusetts. Louise worried that Leonora worked too hard. She could hear the fatigue and discouragement creeping into O'Reilly's writing. So in 1897 she contacted some of her wealthy friends and offered Leonora a deal.

Perkins, Lowell, and others would sponsor Leonora O'Reilly for one year. O'Reilly could leave her factory job. Instead of working for ten tiring, tedious hours every day, she could devote her time to reform activities and finishing her education. Imagine Leonora's reaction. It seemed too good to be true. But these supporters were serious.

O'Reilly left the shirtwaist factory. She felt somewhat disloyal to the workers she oversaw as forewoman, but she'd never have an opportunity like this again. And she hoped that whatever she accomplished outside the factory would help the young women who worked there and at all the other factories.

Leonora and her mother Winifred gave up their small apartment and moved into the Henry Street Settlement for the year. O'Reilly was familiar with the work at Henry Street. In fact, she and Lillian Wald were friends. Once there, Leonora helped with the settlement's investigation of working conditions at sweatshops. And she and one of the settlement's nurses established a women's chapter of the United Garment Workers of America (UGWA), the union that represented workers like herself, her mother, and Rose Schneiderman.

Leonora and Winifred spent many evenings with the other settlement house women. Winifred often told stories and read aloud the works of an Italian revolutionary who she admired. Lillian Wald said later:

> The ardor [enthusiasm] of the daughter continually prodded us to action, and the clear-minded, intelligent mother helped us to a completer [*sic*] realization of the deep-lying causes that had inspired . . . great leaders.[1]

O'Reilly also left the Working Women's Society to start a program she'd been thinking about for some time. A program to help garment workers improve their skills and move up to better-paying jobs. Lillian Wald was always open to ideas and experimentation that might help the people served by the settlement, including the many garment workers who lived nearby. Together, Wald and O'Reilly established the Model Shirtwaist Shop—a very small factory in the attic of the house on Henry Street. The goal was to turn young women who sewed buttons and hems and seams into expert seamstresses who could make elaborate dresses and coats and more. Women with those skills made more money than less skilled workers. They could find better jobs and make greater demands. Winifred O'Reilly had taught Leonora those skills. Now, Leonora would teach a group of young women how to use sewing machines and develop their earning power.

The new sewing room in the Henry Street attic was clean, with good lighting and plenty of room for six women to train on sewing machines. They worked eight-hour days instead of the usual ten, and had an hour for lunch instead of a few minutes. One young woman had come to Henry Street to escape sexual harassment at the garment factory where she worked. When she joined the Model Shirtwaist Shop, she described it as "a dream."[2] In Leonora's mind, the shop was an example of what every garment worker's situation should be.

The young women learned quickly and the shop produced very well-made shirtwaists. But dark, dirty, overcrowded, and unsanitary factories and sweatshops could sell their shirtwaists for less money. Think about the numbers. A place that spent practically nothing on its workers or shops was a bargain for consumers—as long as they didn't think about the germs that spread to the fabrics in those places or what the people who made that clothing suffered.

Sadly, in the end, the Model Shirtwaist Shop couldn't compete. People would continue to buy the cheaper products until most factories paid decent wages. O'Reilly had to close the shop at the end of the year. Everyone felt heartbreak.

Leonora was discouraged, of course. But she didn't give up. Neither did many thousands of women in the garment industry. For now, the eight-hour day, real breaks, and clean, safe conditions remained only a dream. Yet O'Reilly and others were sure that their efforts would pay off. Someday. They just had to keep at it, making progress in small steps.

In the meantime, Leonora O'Reilly had realized that she had a talent for teaching. In the fall of 1898, she enrolled in domestic arts classes at the Pratt Institute in New York. There, she earned her credentials as a sewing instructor and began teaching at the Manhattan Trade School for Girls.

O'Reilly also kept talking. She spoke to women's clubs and workers' groups. She made speeches in auditoriums and outside on street corners. Always dressed in a white shirtwaist and dark skirt, Leonora didn't pretend to be anything other than a working woman. A dignified, intelligent working woman. She gained attention across the country as she stood "gaunt and Irish and pale with the burden of her destiny."[3]

Some people considered O'Reilly an impressive defender of workingwomen even if she didn't behave as "ladies" should. Others saw an "agitator"—someone who stirs up public opinion—and used the term as an insult. Leonora was proud to be both a defender and an agitator as she stood before workers and anyone else who would listen. By 1900, Leonora O'Reilly was a leading spokesperson for workingwomen nationwide. Despite years of tireless work, though, progress seemed almost nonexistent. What more could she do?

The American Federation of Labor (AFL) had become the most powerful labor organization in the country by the start of the twentieth century. It was made up of smaller organizations of skilled workers and intentionally stayed out of politics. The AFL's founder and president, Samuel Gompers, had no interest in changing American government. He believed in capitalism. But not the completely unregulated capitalism that men like Carnegie and Rockefeller and a lot of politicians preached. Gompers believed that skilled workers had the right to join together in unions, the very thing industrialists fought against. United workers could "negotiate"—work out agreements—for better wages, hours, and conditions. They could improve American capitalism without violence or revolution. Everyone could benefit.

Leonora agreed. "We must teach our employers that we are workers with them in the industrial world," she said.[4] But her agreement with the AFL didn't matter. The organization did not admit what they called unskilled workers—men doing jobs that didn't require much experience or training (today these people are called low-wage laborers). And it certainly didn't admit women.

AFL leaders feared that women workers would take jobs away from the men who really needed them. As if women didn't need their jobs. They saw all women workers—even those with good skills—as unskilled and not worth the money men could make. That sounded like what industrialists said. But most union men didn't seem to notice.

Leonora O'Reilly and a number of other women reformers tried to change the organization's views but couldn't. Working together would have been empowering and effective. But the women weren't going to give up. They would form their own organization. Leonora O'Reilly helped to establish the Women's Trade Union League (WTUL) in 1903.

Like the AFL, the Women's Trade Union League represented many industries. But unlike other groups, its founders, leaders, and members were a very diverse collection of women. Many were working class like O'Reilly. They tended to be young and

Women's National Trade Union (WTUL) logo

included a lot of Jewish immigrants from eastern European countries. The rest were mostly Italian and Irish immigrants and largely Catholic.

Full-time reformers such as Lillian Wald and Jane Addams were involved in starting the WTUL too. Most of them were white, middle class, and Protestant (though Wald was Jewish). Wealthy, influential women participated as well. They were generally the daughters or wives of men who were successful in business but believed in reform.[5]

Leonora welcomed everyone's support. But she sometimes resented the attitude she saw among middle-class and wealthy women. They sometimes acted as though they thought they were better than the workingwomen they hoped to help. Most probably didn't even realize it. They simply didn't understand the reality of a working woman's life, just as they didn't understand Leonora's refusal to speak gently.

O'Reilly wasn't alone in criticizing middle-class progressives. Working-class people didn't want pity. They didn't want to be looked down on. They didn't want to become someone they weren't in order to be respected. Leonora understood. She was one of them.

Leonora now supported herself by teaching machine sewing at the Manhattan Trade School for Girls. She didn't have time for the afternoon teas wealthy women often hosted to promote the organization. She was at work during teatime. And she had picket lines to march in, strikes to lead, speeches to write. She had her own housework and laundry and cooking to do as well. Most middle-class women did not.

Leonora O'Reilly didn't hesitate to explain all that to the WTUL's benefactors whenever she thought they needed to hear it. She told a group of college women, "not to correct the grammar of working girls . . . let the girls do things in their own way."[6] She reminded them that workingwomen didn't need to act or speak like well-off women to have worth. They had earned dignity and pride just as they were. O'Reilly was considered "the conscience of the league."[7]

Over the next few years, Leonora and the WTUL supported a women-led strike of sixty thousand garment workers in Chicago. They aided corset makers in Kalamazoo, Michigan. O'Reilly traveled to Michigan for that strike and saw one of her colleagues roughly arrested. The woman was kept in jail for over a month. Had she broken a law? No, but that didn't matter to the powerful men who wanted to intimidate their employees.

Rough tactics, however, often backfired. Women didn't stop marching or striking. In fact, more women organized to make their demands heard. They didn't win very often, but they weren't about to quit. They were determined to make progress, no matter how long it took.

By 1909, Leonora O'Reilly was making speeches almost every day and writing articles for magazines and newspapers as well. All this in addition to the job she now had recruiting women workers to the WTUL. She believed that workingwomen (and men) had to have political power as well as the power to organize in order to improve their working lives. It was all tied together. Marches, parades, and strikes had their place. But the vote was critical. She told a group of workingwomen:

Women's Trade Union League, labor parade, 1908

> Women, whether you wish it or not, your first step must be to gain equal political rights with men. The next step after that must be equal pay for equal work.[8]

Whether they wished it or not? The fact was that many women (and most men) either didn't think about voting rights for women or didn't want women to vote. They had always thought of politics as a man's world, a rough-and-tumble world, as Albion Bacon had. They believed that women were better than that. More virtuous. That they should stay above politics for their own sakes and for their children.

Leonora O'Reilly was ready to change that thinking. To educate women and men. Politicians weren't going to make laws to help workingwomen unless there was something in it for them, votes that would keep them in office. That was reality.

O'Reilly had seen the police abuse picketing women. She'd seen women being arrested for nothing more than walking on the sidewalk. Beaten so badly they were hospitalized. One judge said that the women were "on strike against God and Nature."[9] God and nature didn't want women to be paid enough to feed their children?

O'Reilly wrote:

> "These strikers are the vanguard [leading edge] of the intelligent revolt against our present irrational, barbaric, soulless industrial system."[10]

International Ladies' Garment Workers' Union (ILGWU) strike, 1909–1910

Was the industrial system as bad as all that? A terrible tragedy answered the question.

On a cold Saturday in late March 1911, a fire broke out just before closing time at the Triangle Shirtwaist Factory in Manhattan. The factory took up the eighth, ninth, and tenth floors of the large building. Hundreds of people, mostly Jewish and Italian immigrant women and girls, worked there six days a week. Nearly everything on the factory's three floors—tables, bins, walls, floors, tissue-paper patterns, and thousands of yards of fabric—was easily flammable. In less than five minutes of the first sign of fire, all three stories were engulfed in smoke and flames.

Terrified workers on the eighth and ninth floors raced to the main exit, but the fire blocked their way. They scrambled to a second stairwell but found the doors locked. Factory owners often locked exit doors to keep workers from stealing or taking breaks. Some workers on the tenth floor were able to get to the roof, and students from the building next door raced to help them escape. Other workers crammed into the elevator, whose operator had the courage to make two more trips up and down. Then the elevator collapsed. The one rickety fire escape also collapsed, dropping dozens of workers to their deaths.

Crowds gathered in the street. They never forgot the nightmare they saw. One witness wrote later:

> Horrified and helpless, the crowds – I among them – looked up at the burning building, saw girl after girl appear at the reddened windows, pause for a terrified moment, and then leap to the pavement below . . . The emotions of the crowd were indescribable. Women were hysterical, scores fainted; men wept.[11]

The bodies of the victims were taken to a pier along the East River, where families and friends came to identify the remains of their loved ones. Shock blanketed the city of New York. In all, 146 people—123 of them women garment workers—had died. That was more deaths than any industrial disaster in New York's history. It remains one of the worst industrial disasters in American history today.

The one fire escape, March 25, 1911

The two owners of the factory were brought to trial on charges of "manslaughter"—responsibility for a death, but not murder. The factory had no safety equipment, only one unstable fire escape, locked doors, no alarms, no sprinklers . . . Those precautions would have cost money the owners did not want to spend. Yet the jury found the men not guilty. Imagine how the families of the dead must have felt. Thousands of New Yorkers were outraged.

The state legislature responded by forming a commission to investigate the Triangle Shirtwaist Factory fire. Leonora O'Reilly was part of that commission. The eloquent garment worker knew whereof she spoke. If legislators had listened to warnings and enacted and enforced safety standards, the

Firefighters at the Triangle Shirtwaist Factory, March 25, 1911

tragedy would never have occurred. They were as guilty as the factory owners.

The commission's report led to the passage of more than fifty laws regulating fire safety and factory inspections in New York.

Leonora, with daughter Alice in her lap, and Winifred, around 1907–1911

Those were steps in the right direction. But there was still a long way to go.

O'Reilly continued to speak on behalf of workingwomen through the WTUL. She still chided the upper-class women when they displayed a lack of understanding. But she called many of them friends and considered the organization "women's real togetherness."[12] She also championed women's suffrage and spoke before the US Senate Judiciary Committee in Washington, DC, in 1912:

> I have been a wage earner since I was a little over thirteen. I . . . know whereof I speak . . . You cannot or will not make laws for us; we must make laws for ourselves. We working women need the ballot for self-protection; that is all there is to it. We have got to have it.
>
> . . . the working woman, facing the hard facts of life and having to fight her way, has come to the conclusion that you men in politics . . . are not leaders, you follow what you think is the next step on the ladder.
>
> We working women want the ballot, not as a privilege but as a right.[13]

✣✣✣

Leonora kept up her pace, speaking with fiery energy, organizing labor, leading workingwomen to march with the well-to-do in suffrage parades, and more. She saw the end of legal sweatshops, the beginning of business regulations, and the 1920 passage of the Nineteenth Amendment guaranteeing women's right to vote. But her health had suffered over the years. O'Reilly died of heart failure in 1927 at the age of fifty-seven, still a champion for workingwomen everywhere.

Then, In-Between, and Now: Labor Unions

Then: Enormous companies hired thousands of workers in the late 1800s. This meant that employers and employees no longer personally knew one another or worked together in the same space. Industrialists' drive for profit left workers powerless. They faced long hours, low wages, and dangerous conditions—or no jobs at all. Some workers turned to labor unions—organizations to represent them to their employers as a group.

Early unions found support from middle-class Americans who believed that business owners should treat their workers decently. But these unions lost support when clashes between owners and workers grew violent. Average citizens didn't like it when strikes disrupted railroad travel and the delivery of goods. And the middle class felt real fear of unions when some labor leaders talked about revolution.

Labor organizers didn't give up. Neither did women

and minorities, who were excluded from most unions. Black labor leaders formed the Colored National Labor Union in 1869. Leonora O'Reilly and others pushed to organize garment workers in the 1880s. Luisa Capetillo helped tobacco workers in Puerto Rico organize with the Free Federation of Workers in 1899 (Puerto Rico had become a US territory in 1898).[14] They and many others fought both the tycoons and prejudice.

The American Federation of Labor brought together many different labor unions in one organization. Thousands of workers joined. The AFL was not violent or political. But like most earlier unions, it did not admit women, Irish and Italian immigrants (because they were usually Catholic), or Black workers. By 1914, the AFL had grown to two million members. They had made some gains in wages and hours. Along with other unions and progressive reformers, the AFL had convinced Congress to establish the Department of Labor. Its mission was to promote the welfare of American workers. Even so, less than 15 percent of all American workers belonged to unions in 1914.

In-Between: The US economy collapsed in 1929. The nation (and much of the world) fell into the worst economic depression in history. Businesses failed. Millions of working-class and middle-class Americans lost their jobs, their homes, and their savings. As the Great Depression worsened, many people questioned democracy and capitalism. Citizens in some countries turned to revolution or to fascism. Voters in the United States overwhelmingly elected Democrat Franklin Roosevelt president in 1932. Roosevelt's programs were known as the New Deal. Under the New Deal, Congress established Social Security to guarantee working Americans some retirement income. It passed laws protecting workers' right to form unions and bargain with employers. Other laws established a minimum wage and banned child labor. Union membership grew rapidly. And Roosevelt's secretary of labor, Frances Perkins, was the first woman to serve in a presidential cabinet.

About one-third of American workers belonged to unions by the mid-1950s. Their wages, negotiated by unions in their contracts, put them in the middle class. And they were more likely to have retirement funds, health insurance, and other benefits than non-union workers. All the while, business owners continued to oppose unions.

Union membership peaked in 1955. By then, 35 percent of American workers belonged to unions. Union membership numbers stayed high through the 1960s.[15] During that time, the government expanded safety nets, with programs including Medicare to provide health insurance for retired people. And new groups of workers organized. Migrant farm workers who move from one fruit or vegetable harvest to another were (and still are) some of the most exploited laborers in the US. Migrant workers in California, most of them Mexican American, organized the National Farm Workers Association (now the United Farm Workers) in 1962. They used strikes, boycotts, and nonviolent protests to achieve bargaining agreements with employers.

Business owners argued that giving in to labor's

demands would harm the economy. They feared that giving workers high wages and benefits would keep their companies from competing against foreign businesses that didn't have such costs. They feared smaller profits for themselves and their investors. But the economy of the 1950s and '60s remained strong. One reason was that union workers could now afford to buy the products they and other workers were making. Businesses benefited as much as workers did as they sold more goods.

Now: Business leaders regained political influence and power during the late 1960s and 1970s. They supported political candidates who opposed labor laws. Over time, they succeeded in getting some of those laws repealed. Without as many government protections for unions, membership has declined. As of 2023, just 10 percent of American workers belong to unions.[16] That is a lower rate than in 1914. And in recent years, workers have reported intimidation of workers who try to start or join unions at major companies, including Amazon and Starbucks.[17]

As unions have declined, the wealth gap has increased. Middle-class and working-class families now face more financial risk than they did during the 1950s and '60s. Yet a 2023 report from the US Department of Treasury indicates that unions can have a positive impact on these trends. Where unions are strong, workers tend to be more economically stable and have higher wages and better working conditions.[18]

Today, the trend away from unions may be shifting again, along with public opinion. Polls conducted in

2025 indicate that nearly 70 percent of Americans approve of unions.[19]

And so: The natural tension between employees and employers raises a lot of questions. Where is the balance between fair wages and working conditions for employees on the one hand, and the ability of business owners to make a profit on the other? Do unions make unreasonable demands on business owners? And what is the government's role in all this? Should government protect the right of workers to join unions? When does regulation become an unfair or unreasonable burden on business owners? Perhaps most important, who defines that?

CHAPTER 13

"Never Frown, Never Sigh"

Sarah Chase Harris was twenty-two years old when her very comfortable middle-class world fell apart. Two years earlier, she had married a merchant, or store owner, in her hometown of Holyoke, Massachusetts. Charles Harris was about ten years older than Sarah and was able to buy a nice house and good furniture for the two of them. They received lovely wedding gifts too. And Sarah's mother gave her "heirlooms"—linens and silver and other items that had been in her family for a long time.

Sarah took on her role as a wife and also volunteered with a group that helped the poor of the city. She'd been doing that for some time even before she married. Everything seemed just right. A good husband, a lovely home, interests of her own, perhaps children one day . . .

Then Charles Harris died suddenly. The man Sarah had planned to spend her life with was dead. That was a very difficult thing to accept. But before Sarah had time to think about life without Charles, she got more bad news. She was about to lose almost everything they had owned as a couple—her house, her furniture, her wedding gifts, even her family treasures. How? Why?

States have laws regulating what happens to a person's property when that person dies. In Massachusetts in the late 1800s, the law said that when a woman married, her property became her husband's property (the husband "owned" even the couple's children). When a married man died, his widow received only one-third of his property. His parents and siblings got the other two-thirds. Because of this law, Sarah had to move out of the house Charles had bought for them. Most of the furniture went to his family. Sarah's mother's linens and silver went too. So did most of the wedding gifts.

How was Sarah Chase Harris supposed to live? As a middle-class young woman, she couldn't simply go find a job. She definitely couldn't buy a house. Did Charles's family, the Harrises, see the injustice? They were supposed to be *her* family as well as his now. But they took her possessions anyway. There was nothing she could do about it.

Sarah was beyond grief, beyond anger. As much as she had loved Charles, she refused to use the Harris name ever again. She'd go back to being Sarah Chase. Back to being a single young woman in a world where single young women could fall into poverty in an instant. This was Sarah Chase's awakening. Her awakening to the legal inequality American women faced.

Despite her grief, Sarah couldn't focus on the past. Constant sadness or bitterness weren't in her nature. She would move back home with her parents and near her siblings (she was the fifth of seven children). She would continue her volunteer work and go on—somehow. Later in life, she'd say that her motto was, "Never frown, never sigh, keep step."[1]

Several years later, Sarah Chase met a doctor and had the courage to fall in love again. James Platt was more than fifteen years older than Sarah. He'd practiced medicine in Vermont before volunteering for the US Army during the Civil War. He had then served three terms in the US House of Representatives and eventually settled in New York. When he and Sarah married in 1884, he was living in the Queens borough of New York City. He directed a children's home—what some people called an orphanage. Sarah soon began working at the home as a volunteer.

Mrs. Sarah Platt Decker, around 1904

"Civic life"—activities that promote the well-being of the community—was ingrained in Sarah's family. Her mother was part of the same family as United States founders John Adams and Samuel Adams. More recent ancestors had worked to end slavery. Sarah herself had served on the board of trustees of the local charity in Holyoke. Her new work at the children's home in Queens began a lifelong commitment to child welfare. That commitment deepened when her daughter Harriet was born in 1885.

In 1887, James and Sarah decided to leave New York and move nearly two thousand miles west to Denver, Colorado. Imagine the adventure of traveling by train across a thousand miles of the Great Plains and arriving in Denver to see mountain peaks more than twice as high as any on the East Coast.

The move opened a new chapter in Sarah's life. Denver, the capital of Colorado, was an exciting place to be in the late 1800s. No one person was making the rules for society the way

Caroline Astor did in New York. No one in Colorado could say they'd *always* done something a certain way, as happened in Boston and other Eastern cities. Denver was still too young for that.

Less than thirty years earlier, Denver had been a small mining settlement in the brand-new territory of Colorado. The few people who lived there weren't sure the town would even survive as other mining towns sprang up. But forward-thinking businessmen and the Colorado Territory's early governors brought a new railroad line to Denver, and the small town became the central point for transportation and trade in all directions.

In 1870, Denver had been home to fewer than five thousand people. By the time the Platt family arrived seventeen years later, Colorado had become a state (in 1876) with Denver as its capital, and the city's population had grown to over one hundred thousand.

The rapid growth in population and business brought wealth to a number of Denverites and turned the little town into a real city. Soon after James and Sarah moved there, the impressive State Capitol Building was completed. It stood atop a central hill and marked the city's official elevation—5,280 feet, or exactly one mile above sea level. Theaters, an opera house, and luxury hotels dotted the wide downtown streets.

The city didn't have as many millionaires as New York, of course. But the Denverites who had wealth were just as eager to build mansions as anyone in New York or Chicago or elsewhere.

Once in Colorado, James Platt set aside his medical career and built a paper mill. He was very successful and quickly became a prominent member of the community. Sarah got involved in the city as well. Outgoing and likeable, she was also direct and practical. Denver suited her.

✤✤✤

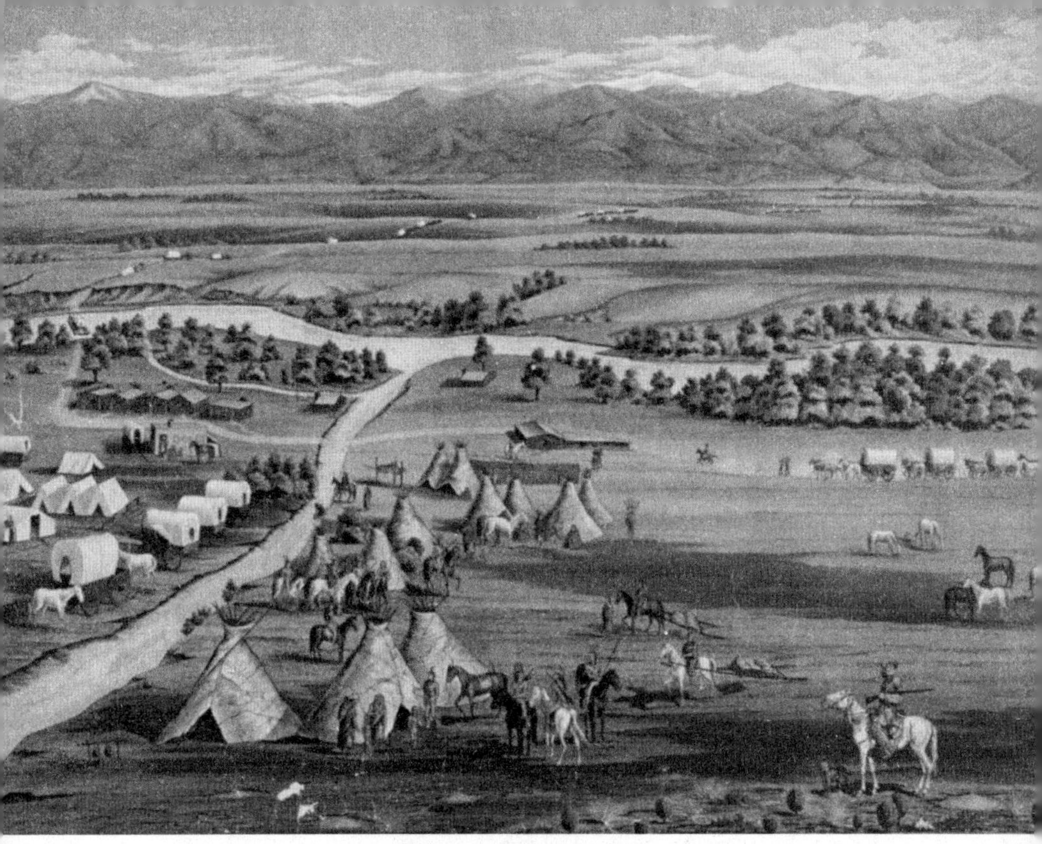

Painting of Denver, Colorado, 1859

Denver's rapid growth had resulted in urban problems as well as prosperity. That was no surprise. It was the same thing that had happened in other American cities. But like other cities, the middle class was growing too, and many members of that middle class were determined to solve their city's problems—corruption in state and city government, big crime bosses, dirty and dangerous streets, poverty, lack of sanitation, overcrowding in poorer areas, and more. Sarah Platt began doing volunteer work as soon as she, James, and Harriet were settled. She expanded that work when the city fell on hard times.

The Panic of 1893—the economic depression that caused so much unemployment in New York City and across the country—hit Denver especially hard. A drought brought misery to ranchers and farmers, who could not pay their debts. Then silver mines

Denver, Colorado, around 1898

all over Colorado closed, and thousands of miners lost their jobs. The Union Pacific Railroad declared bankruptcy, banks failed, and their customers lost all their savings. Businesses went under.

Hundreds and then thousands of unemployed men came to Denver looking for aid. Sarah Platt helped organize relief for them and their families. She worked with the city government to set up a tent camp for the homeless. That was good, necessary, practical work. And Sarah earned a lot of praise for her efforts and her organizational skills. But relief efforts were only one of many things she was busy with in 1893.

Providing the needy with shelter and food was an act of charity. It was desperately important, and Platt was glad she could help. But as Jacob Schiff and Lillian Wald in New York understood, charity didn't change the structure of society.

It didn't solve the causes of poverty. It wasn't reform. And it wasn't the kind of change Sarah Platt had wanted for fifteen years—ever since her dark days in Holyoke when her first husband died.

Laws restricting women and what property they could or could not own were unfair. Unreasonable. Sarah Platt had learned that firsthand. But men made the laws. Most men wouldn't listen to even the best argument if that argument came from a woman. Why not? The men who made the laws wanted votes, and women had no vote.

Like Leonora O'Reilly, Platt was certain that the only way to make the laws fair for women was to guarantee women the right to vote—suffrage. She saw a real possibility of achieving that in Colorado.

American women had been working for suffrage for fifty

years. They'd been laughed at and shut out and ignored. Sometimes by other women. But Sarah felt a difference in Colorado. Maybe it was the newness of the mountain states. Maybe it was a desire to attract more women to move there. Maybe it was simply recognition of women's strength and determination. After all, a lot of women in the Rocky Mountain states had come in wagon trains across the blistering heat and bone-chilling cold of the Great Plains. How could anyone say they were too frail or too delicate to participate in democracy?

Colorado's neighbors had already acknowledged a woman's right to vote. Wyoming approved it in 1869 (before it became a state in 1890). And Utah (still a territory in 1893) passed a women's suffrage bill in 1870. When Colorado became a state in 1876 and wrote its state constitution, efforts were made to include women's suffrage. Those efforts failed. Another vote on suffrage came up in 1877. That "referendum"—a direct vote by eligible voters on a law or other political question—had the governor's support. The most famous leaders of the suffrage movement, including Susan B. Anthony, traveled to Colorado to campaign for passage of the referendum. Anthony bounced from one town to another by train and stagecoach and made speeches to friendly and unfriendly audiences. Still, the measure failed.

Men who owned saloons and breweries opposed women's suffrage because many women wanted to pass anti-alcohol or "temperance" laws. They didn't want those women to have the vote. Miners didn't like the idea of change. And "Hispanos" (the descendants of Mexicans who had lived in southern Colorado when the land was still part of Mexico) opposed changes to their long-standing traditions.[2]

But now, more than a decade later, women's suffrage supporters saw the same thing Sarah Platt did—an opportunity to try again, this time successfully. The key was a well-organized campaign. A group called the Non-Partisan Equal Suffrage Association revised the earlier referendum with the help of a male lawyer. Then Sarah Platt and others talked to newspaper editors and journalists to gain their endorsements and help spread the word.

Sarah also spoke publicly about the referendum. Always with confidence, humor, passion, and common sense. Audiences might wonder at a woman speaking in public. But they liked Sarah, and most people liked what she had to say. She and other women stood for hours at public events and busy markets and any place where they could encourage people to sign petitions endorsing equal suffrage. Would all that work be enough?

Think about the challenge these women faced. Who was going to actually vote on this referendum? Men. Only men. No woman in the state was allowed to vote. Platt and the others had to get a majority of male voters to support women's suffrage.

Sarah and her companions weren't deterred. They just kept at it. When the votes were counted on November 7, 1893, the referendum for equal suffrage for men and women had passed by six thousand votes. Those women, who up until that point had no voting power, had achieved something remarkable.

There were still no women in the state legislature or in any other office, but the door had been pushed open. Colorado was now the second state in the United States with full voting rights for women (Utah would become a state in 1896). And it was the first state where women won their right to vote by referendum. The all-male voters of the state had said *yes*. One newspaper gave Sarah Platt "a great share of the credit."[3]

✤✤✤

Sarah Platt had seen her dream become reality. But what about her concerns for child welfare? And juvenile justice? And laws to protect women's property? And votes for women in other states? And better schools? And so much more . . .

CHAPTER 14

★★★

"Keep Step"

Getting the vote was an enormous victory for women in Colorado and for Sarah Platt personally. But she believed that the challenge now was to make sure that women used their new power to demand changes in society. Changes that would protect women and children and improve their lives. Sarah devoted herself to the work, even though her own life didn't seem to need much improvement at all. She was doing it for others.

Platt had come a long way since losing everything when Charles Harris died. Perhaps most important, she'd found love again. James Platt was a good man. They had a wonderful daughter and had made friends in Denver. And Platt's paper mill business was remarkably successful. They now lived in a neighborhood on Capitol Hill where millionaires had built huge homes. James purchased a gigantic stone house called Castle Marne. Imagine that. Practical, energetic, businesslike Sarah Platt lived in a house meant to look like a castle. It even had a ballroom on the third floor. But wealth didn't change Sarah, or her commitment to reform. She was busier than ever.

In the midst of helping the unemployed and campaigning for equal suffrage, Platt had taken an interest in the women's clubs of Denver. She realized that their members had great potential to become agents of change. "Activists." Club-women could do the practical work of reform. They just needed a push.

Castle Marne, Denver, Colorado

Clubs and associations had been part of American life from the founding of the country. When the French writer and historian Alexis de Tocqueville traveled throughout the United States in the 1830s, he noticed how many associations existed everywhere he went. He wrote:

> In no country in the world has the principle of association been more successfully used, or more [freely] applied to . . . different [purposes], than in America.[1]

There were anti-slavery associations, temperance associations, boating and yacht clubs, chess clubs, hunting clubs, and more. Early women's clubs tended to focus on literary and educational goals for their members. And churches across the country sponsored Bible reading clubs and service organizations.

By the late 1800s, thousands of middle-class women belonged to local women's clubs. Most of these women had more education than their mothers or grandmothers. Many would have gone to college if they'd had the money and opportunity, but most colleges did not admit women until much later. Instead, they turned to clubs for discussions of significant books and plays. They invited experts to talk about topics from literature to history to preparing healthy meals for their families. Women in cities and towns across the country took part in these clubs for the intellectual offerings and as a way to meet other women, make friends, and share ideas and sometimes struggles.

As the twentieth century drew near, however, some clubwomen felt a need to do more than improve their own intellectual and social lives. They saw the divisions and dangers in the country—labor unrest, radical union leaders talking of revolution, corruption in state and federal government, urban poverty and disease—and decided to make real efforts at reform outside their traditional domestic spheres.

Sarah Platt saw this shift taking place and hoped to build on it. She wanted to move the women's clubs of Denver toward reform. Many clubs did participate in some efforts already. But they could do more. They could engage in down-to-earth reform work. Pragmatic work. Effective work. Women in Colorado now had political power that most American women still only dreamed of. They should use it.

Platt and a group of like-minded women founded the Women's Club of Denver (WCD) in 1894, soon after the equal suffrage bill passed. But it wasn't one single club. It was a group of clubs. A club of clubs. Each individual group could maintain its own membership and focus. But the WCD would offer collective information on important issues and opportunities. A club of twenty women could have only so much influence. Think how much dozens of clubs with different kinds of experience could do together.

Sarah Platt was well known and well respected in Denver.

Many women had heard her speak in support of equal suffrage. She'd been a key figure in getting that bill passed. She was also the woman who'd organized help for desperate unemployed men and their families and was still doing so. And she served on the boards of several local organizations dealing with the justice system and child labor. Members of the new Women's Club of Denver trusted her. She was smart and funny and always positive. They elected Sarah Platt to be the WCD's first president.

In August of that same year, Sarah, James, and Harriet decided to have a short holiday from their busy lives and spend some time together as a family. They took the train to Georgetown, Colorado, and stayed at a hotel on Green Lake in the mountains about fifty miles west of Denver.

On the last day of their vacation, James Platt went to the lake for a little fly-fishing. He'd been out only a short time when people on the shore saw him stand up in his small boat and suddenly fall forward into the water. Several men raced to rescue him. They got to Platt and pulled him onto the sand very quickly, but he died moments later. There was nothing anyone could do. A newspaper described Sarah as "beside herself with grief."[2]

Doctors later determined that James Platt had not drowned. He'd had a stroke. That was why he'd fallen into the water. It didn't really matter. For the second time, Sarah's life was shattered. At just thirty-nine, she was a widow again, this time with a young child to raise.

Property laws in Colorado were not like the laws in Massachusetts had been seventeen years earlier. There was no such thing as the "widow's third." Platt now owned Castle Marne and all the investments and possessions she and James had. She would rather have James than any possession, of course. But at least she wasn't going to be left with practically nothing for herself or her daughter.

Sarah soon sold Castle Marne. She and nine-year-old Harriet had no need or desire to stay in the big mansion. Platt was much too involved in her reform work to look after such a place. And she needed to move on. "Never frown, never sigh, keep step." No matter how hard that was.

Platt threw herself into her role as president of the Women's Club of Denver. She'd have to "keep step" if she was going to give local women's clubs the push that she thought some needed. She spoke to individual clubs and encouraged members to embrace the wide view of the domestic sphere that Albion Bacon, Lugenia Hope, and other progressive women inhabited. She told them that "women's work" included making their communities better places to live. With that in mind, she organized committees within the WCD to look at public health issues and city services like garbage collection and streetlights throughout the city, not just in the center of town. Other committees would focus on temperance, legislation, and government work or "civil service" (Congress had passed the Civil Service Act of 1871, requiring that federal workers be hired based on their skills, not as favors from politicians, though the act didn't apply to local governments).[3]

The various clubs took on projects that their members cared about. The clubwomen opened nursery schools in Denver, looked for ways to get medical care for the poor, and established safe playgrounds and traveling libraries. Most members found the work fulfilling and educational as they learned the skills they needed to accomplish their goals. That was common among progressive women. Like Albion Bacon, they weren't experts when they started their reform efforts. But they became experts in order to get the job done.

The Women's Club of Denver joined the General Federation

of Women's Clubs (GFWC)—a nationwide organization founded in New York in 1890. As president of the Denver branch, Platt traveled to Kentucky for the 1896 GFWC convention. She gave a speech there about the kind of work she believed women's clubs should be doing and got a very positive response. The spirit of reform had spread widely.

Two years later, the convention came to Denver. Platt organized the event and spoke again, this time gaining national attention. Before the convention ended, the delegates had passed a resolution condemning child labor and calling for laws against it. They also elected Sarah Platt as their national vice president. But when members approached her about running for president of the GFWC in 1902, she said no.

Sarah knew that she would have to travel all over the country as president of the GFWC. The time was not right for that. She had married again in 1899, about five years after James Platt's death. Westbrook Decker, a longtime friend, was a judge in Denver. But after their marriage he had needed to retire because of poor health. Sarah wanted to stay close to home. In 1903, a few months after Sarah had been asked to run for president of the GFWC, Judge Decker died of pneumonia, leaving Sarah Platt Decker a widow for the third time. She was forty-eight years old.

Sarah took a deep breath and forged on. Again. Harriet was nearly twenty now and didn't need her mother at home. So when Sarah had a second opportunity to lead the GFWC, it was a dream come true. She accepted the position as president of the GFWC in 1904 and went to work.

Mrs. Decker, as she was called then, spent hundreds of hours on trains going from one city or town to another. She wanted to hear from the women's clubs in different parts of the country. Decker spoke, but she also listened. She visited twenty-six state conventions in her first two-year term as president of the GFWC. Wherever she went, she encouraged clubwomen to make the shift from literary and social groups to clubs that worked to improve the world around them.[4] Discussions of classical literature were fine. But it was time to discuss the issues clubwomen saw in their own hometowns every day.

"Ladies," she said to the women at the 1904 convention:

> Dante [an Italian poet of the Middle Ages] is dead. He died several centuries ago, and a great many things have happened since his time. Let us drop the study of his *Inferno* [a lengthy poem] and proceed in earnest to contemplate our own social order.[5]

Decker didn't nag. She didn't make anyone feel guilty for not doing enough. She spoke with good cheer, laughed at herself, and talked about the power women could have.

Sarah also studied the work that was already taking place across the state. Many women's clubs were acting on a variety of local issues, from garbage collection to nursery schools. Clubwomen viewed those kinds of reforms as within the domestic sphere—important to the health and well-being of their families and neighborhoods. An astonishing number of clubs had also worked miracles for isolated families and nearby communities with no access to books. Reading, of course, was an enormous part of education. And education was another part of the domestic sphere, and a woman's responsibility. Plus, it made sense that women who first came together to discuss books would want to share the joy and benefits of reading with others.

Picture living in a tiny mining camp in western Montana, or in a windswept farmhouse on the Great Plains in Oklahoma.

Imagine living there in the days before the internet, before television, before radio, before the telephone. One day, a mule-drawn wagon arrives. It's filled with books that anyone can borrow for free. Simply return them the next time the wagon comes, then borrow more. For men, women, and children with no access to reading materials, those books were a lifeline to education and entertainment, and an escape from their day-to-day lives.

Women's clubs all over the United States were responsible for these traveling libraries. Big cities and towns had established public libraries by the late 1800s. Some even funded traveling libraries to serve people who couldn't get to a library building. But small towns and rural areas didn't have enough tax money to do that. Women's clubs filled the gap.

The clubs held bake sales and tag sales and everything else they could think of to raise money. Volunteers collected donated books and decided which others to buy (based on their own ideas about what books were appropriate and acceptable). They organized and cataloged the books. And then they set off in wagons or carts to bring their mobile libraries to the people who needed them. During the early 1900s, women's clubs in Illinois alone ran three hundred traveling libraries. Clubs from Maine to Montana did the same (today, local governments fund traveling libraries—often called bookmobiles). A study of thirty-four states where the GFWC had clubs counted over 4,600 traveling libraries and more than 340,000 books.[6]

Clubwomen also lobbied local governments to fund libraries, often with help from Andrew Carnegie. The steel tycoon used his fortune to build libraries in towns and cities across the country (and in Europe). He built a library in almost any town or city that agreed to pay for books and librarians' salaries. Women's clubs usually raised that money.

However, some towns such as Wheeling, West Virginia,

refused to accept Carnegie's building funds. Men who had worked in Carnegie's mills, and their families, saw Carnegie as a danger to the workers who had made him wealthy rather than a benefactor. In 1904, Wheeling rejected the offered grant. Think about that. Those families would rather have no library at all than one built by Andrew Carnegie. Later, the city's Board of Education raised money and opened a public library in 1911.[7]

Even so, Carnegie built over two thousand libraries in the United States. Most were beautifully designed and stood as monuments to learning.[8]

In 1933, the American Library Association estimated that three-fourths of all the libraries then in existence in the US had been built through the efforts of America's clubwomen and their

Carnegie Library, Washington, DC, 1910

"zealous and persistent work."[9] That's an impressive statistic. But like the member clubs of the GFWC and other clubs, most of those libraries were open only to white people.

As the nation entered the twentieth century, women in most states still couldn't vote regardless of their race or status. But men in some states had elected progressive legislators and governors (all men, of course). That opened the door for clubwomen and others to promote progressive state laws and policies such as Albion Bacon's housing law in Indiana. However, some issues required action from the federal government in Washington, DC.

Could clubwomen in Butte, Montana, or Bangor, Maine, or Biloxi, Mississippi, actually influence the federal government? Women like Sarah Platt Decker thought they could. Fittingly, a book convinced them to try.

CHAPTER 15

For Better and Worse

Upton Sinclair was a muckraker. Like Jacob Riis and other progressive journalists, writers, and photographers, he worked to expose corruption and wrongdoing in business and government. Sinclair wanted to raise awareness and stir up anger about conditions in the meatpacking industry. So he spent several weeks working undercover in Chicago to see firsthand what the workers in the stockyards and meat-processing plants suffered. Then he put the terrible details into a novel called *The Jungle*, published in 1905. He hoped that readers would feel strongly enough to demand change for exploited workers. Just as Jacob Riis had hoped people who saw his photographs would demand change for the poor in New York City.

The Jungle succeeded in stirring up anger—enormous anger. More anger than Sinclair had imagined. Middle-class readers felt outrage and fury. But they weren't thinking about workers or labor reform. They were thinking about just one part of the book.

Imagine reading descriptions of coughing, hacking workers packaging meat with their bare hands. Picture how readers shuddered at the idea that diseased cows were slaughtered and sold as

In the heart of the Union Stockyards, Chicago, Illinois, around 1909

roasts. Or gagged when they read about rat droppings and whole rats—and sometimes human fingers—going into meat grinders with the beef or pork that ended up in their kitchens. Men falling into huge vats where they became part of the blocks of lard—supposedly pork fat—sold in groceries.[1]

The middle class, many of them clubwomen, wanted answers. They now knew they'd been buying and feeding their families dangerous, diseased food. They wanted reform. Food safety reform. As Sinclair said, "I aimed at the public's heart, and by accident I hit it in the stomach."[2]

Homemakers weren't to blame for buying unhealthy, contaminated products. At the start of the twentieth century, canned and boxed and jarred food had no ingredients labels at all. Was that peanut butter really made of peanuts? Were the strawberries in that jam coated in some sort of insect repellent? Was there sawdust in that bread? There was no way of knowing.

No one inspected meat or fish or other animal products either. Had a meatpacker filled the sausages with rat meat? Did the dairy add chalk, or worse, formaldehyde—a highly poisonous gas—to the milk? And how long had that fish been out of water before it went into a can?

Other muckrakers exposed the dangers in nonfood products too. Children's cough medicine often included opium—an addictive and sometimes deadly drug. The main ingredient in widely advertised vitamin syrups was alcohol.

Diseased meat? Chalk-filled milk? Opium for infants? Leaving all this to private industry wasn't working. And there wasn't much that local and state governments could do, since products crossed many state lines before they got to a neighborhood market. Only the federal government had the power to take effective action.

Sarah Platt Decker called the General Federation of Women's Clubs "an army of builders, ready, alert, systematic, and scientific."[3] In 1906, they took on a nationwide campaign that proved their power.

Clubwomen had become experts at letter-writing campaigns. Now they used their numbers (the GFWC had nearly eight hundred thousand members by then[4]) to spread the word to fellow clubwomen and everyone else. They must demand federal food safety regulations, meat inspection, and more.

Letters and telegrams flooded into congressional offices and the White House. Writers from all over the country sent the same message. Something had to be done. President Theodore Roosevelt agreed, especially after an investigation showed that Sinclair's descriptions were accurate.[5] Some large food corporations supported federal regulations too. Why? Those companies decided it would be easier to deal with one set of federal regulations across the country rather than individual state regulations that would vary from one place to another. And regulations might cost enough to push small companies out of business and leave the big companies with even more customers.

Within a year, Congress passed the Pure Food and Drug Act and the Meat Inspection Act of 1906. Offices in the Department of Agriculture would enforce the new laws as the Pure Food Bureau.

Support for the bill had been nationwide. But the head of the new bureau gave the GFWC credit for the passage of the laws. "Trust them to put the ball over the goal line every time,"

US marshal destroying worm-infested currants and raisins seized in Washington, DC, bakeries, November 20, 1909

he said.[6] Even if their concerns focused on their families' food rather than the horrific conditions meatpackers faced every day.

Statistics on the impact of the new regulations are difficult to gather. Few records were kept in those days. But according to the National Institutes of Health, deaths from food-borne illnesses such as typhoid fever declined rapidly after 1906.

Passage of the Pure Food and Drug Act was a huge victory for progressive clubwomen. They felt confident that they could do even more. Fortunately, they had an ally in Theodore Roosevelt.

Theodore Roosevelt, 1907

Theodore Roosevelt was a progressive Republican from New York. As governor there, he supported laws to protect laborers, regulate banks, and enlarge the state's park and forestry programs. A majority of New Yorkers liked his ideas, but very conservative Republicans—those who wanted a market economy (capitalism) without regulations—did not. And many were unhappy that he was elected vice president in 1900 when William McKinley ran for and won a second term as president.

Still, some conservative Republicans were pleased with Roosevelt's election. Why? Vice presidents have no specific duties under the Constitution. They often fade into the background after taking office. Opponents of Roosevelt's progressive ideas wanted exactly that for the new vice president. They hoped that the vice presidency would keep him and his views out of the public eye. But just six months after McKinley's 1901 inauguration, a radical "anarchist"—someone who opposes all government—shot the president as he greeted hundreds of people in Buffalo, New York.

Vice President Roosevelt was on vacation when he got the news that McKinley was near death. By the time he got to Buffalo, the president had died. Theodore Roosevelt was now the nation's twenty-sixth president and, at forty-two years old, the youngest president in the nation's history.

Republicans who opposed unions and government regulations were horrified. So were the industrialist tycoons who supported those Republicans. They thought that a progressive in the White House would be a disaster. As Cornelius Vanderbilt IV wrote, "The party was over."[7]

Roosevelt actually kept several of McKinley's policies and most of his advisors. But he didn't hesitate to move the presidency in a new direction. He pushed for policies and laws to protect consumers and children, including the Children's Bureau that Lillian Wald supported. And he was happy to sign the new Pure Food and Drug Act. But conservation of natural resources sat right at the top of Roosevelt's priorities list.

Roosevelt loved the outdoors. He'd been sickly as a child growing up in a wealthy family in New York City. Exercise and time outside helped him overcome serious asthma and other ailments. As president, he went for strenuous hikes in Washington, DC's Rock Creek Park. He insisted that visiting dignitaries hike with him through creeks and mud and anything else.

Theodore Roosevelt had seen more of the United States than most Americans. He'd spent time in the Dakota Territory and even owned a cattle ranch for a while as a young man. He was a horseman and a hunter. He read about the outdoors, the parks, the forests, the grasslands (he was known to read an entire book every day, even as president). He also wrote books on his experiences with nature.

Roosevelt understood that the country's beauty and resources wouldn't last forever without protection. Industrialists were "clear-cutting"—cutting down every tree in an area—one forest after another. Oil tycoons were drilling wells everywhere there might be a chance of finding "black gold." Mine owners were blasting away whole mountainsides in their search for wealth. All these activities were profitable but left the land prone to erosion, water pollution, the loss of wildlife, and more. Roosevelt was eager to stop the irresponsible destruction of the nation's resources—whether the captains of industry liked it or not.

During his first term, Roosevelt established Crater Lake National Park in Oregon. He designated a federal bird reserve in Florida and a federal game preserve in Oklahoma. He also established the US Forest Service to oversee the nation's forests and grasslands. By the time he left office in 1909, Roosevelt had established several more national parks and monuments and forests—over two hundred million acres of protected land in all. Put together, that land was nearly twice the size of California.

Roosevelt held a conservation conference in the spring of 1908. He invited all of the country's governors to come to Washington to discuss natural resources and how they should be used. He also invited experts in conservation from inside and outside the government. Only one woman received an invitation to the conference—Mrs. Sarah Platt Decker, president of the General Federation of Women's Clubs.

Why would President Roosevelt invite the head of an organization of women's clubs to a conference of governors? Because Decker belonged there. The women of the GFWC were now leaders in the conservation movement. Most clubwomen couldn't vote for Roosevelt, of course. But they had influenced many of his conservation decisions.

Laura Lyon White was one of those influential clubwomen. She and her husband had moved from the Great Plains of Iowa to the gold rush hills of California in 1859 to open a general store at the foot of the mountains.

The area should have been a beautiful place to live. But hydraulic mining had ruined the mountain landscape, the water, and the air. Huge jets of water were shot into the rock to break down minerals. The water then moved the dirt or sediment into sluice boxes, where miners sifted for small bits of precious gold metal. Mining companies made massive profits. They also caused massive destruction to mountains, forests, streams, and wildlife.

When scarlet fever (the same disease that Albion Bacon's daughters survived) took the lives of Laura White's two young children, she was certain that pollution caused by the mining had contributed to the tragedy. She and her husband moved to San Francisco for a fresh start. But Laura couldn't leave her tragic experience behind. She began writing articles for magazines and journals. She wanted people to learn and do something about the misuse of natural resources. It wasn't just beauty being lost to industry. It was lives.

Eventually, White founded the California Club and then co-founded the California Federation of Women's Clubs. They soon became part of the GFWC. Like other state federations of women's clubs, the California clubs worked for reforms in schools, juvenile courts, state mental hospitals, housing, and more—all with White's support (sadly, she also supported keeping those clubs segregated). But her real passion was conservation.

The ancient sequoia and redwood trees near the Whites' San Francisco home were among the oldest and largest trees in the world. Some of them had probably been there for more than two thousand years. They stood over three hundred feet tall—the height of a twenty-five-story building. Lumbermen saw the giant trees as a source of giant profits. They wanted to turn the unique, ancient trunks into planks of wood like any other kind of tree. Think about that. Irreplaceable beauty gone forever.

Laura White stepped in to stop them. She gathered thousands of signatures on petitions asking the federal government to protect the Calaveras Big Trees. Congress supported saving the trees, but the man who owned the land where the forests stood refused to sell his property to the government.

While that battle went on, White worked to save the coastal redwoods near Yosemite National Park. They, too, were

"Save the Redwoods." These women were a part of the movement that helped preserve redwoods across the state of California.

endangered by loggers. She started another nationwide effort to preserve those trees. Member clubs of the GFWC answered her call for letters and petitions.

Theodore Roosevelt responded by declaring a section of Redwood Canyon a national monument. He named it for John Muir, the famous naturalist who had introduced him to the redwoods in Yosemite in 1903. The Muir Woods would be a government-protected site.[8] People could travel there to see the redwoods, but they would not be able to destroy the trees. But "people" meant white people. Like the other national parks and monuments, the Muir Woods was segregated. Roosevelt and Muir supported that policy (the parks were finally opened to everyone in 1950).

Laura White and tens of thousands of other clubwomen had succeeded. And though White died in 1916 at the age of seventy-six and didn't live to see her success with the Calaveras Big Trees, she won there, too. In 1931, California established the Calaveras Big Trees State Park. Both parks continue to protect their trees today and have acknowledged and apologized for their earlier racist policies.

Women's clubs in Arizona lobbied to make the Grand Canyon a national park. In Idaho, it was Sawtooth National Park. Florida's Federation of Women's Clubs raised money and awareness to save the wetlands. They became Everglades National Park in 1947. GFWC members took on the protection of ancient Ancestral Puebloan cliff dwellings in Colorado—the remarkable ruins of communities who lived on the cliffsides for more than seven centuries. In 1906, the area was designated Mesa Verde National Park. Today, it is a World Heritage Site, where over a thousand native plant and animal species are protected.

The list of parks and forests goes on. These places weren't

Muir Woods

Mesa Verde National Park

just pretty. They were important for preserving wildlife and plant species, for history, for air quality, flood control, and more.

Other groups also lobbied for conservation projects. For example, a women's branch of the Audubon Society took action when the popularity of feathered hats threatened many species of birds. With help from the GFWC, they succeeded in educating women about the real cost of decorating hats with

Woman wearing a chanticleer hat made of bird feathers, around 1912

exotic bird feathers. Those birds would soon be gone forever if the fashion trend continued. It had happened to other animal species. The clubwomen persuaded Congress to approve a ban on imported wild bird feathers. That ban saved several nearly extinct species, including the beautiful white egret.

After these successes, the GFWC realized that it was time to do more than save land and wildlife bit by bit. They organized a huge campaign demanding that the federal government set up an agency to care for the nation's parks. President Woodrow Wilson, a Democrat, signed the act establishing the National Park Service in 1916.

Sarah Decker stepped down from her leadership of the GFWC in 1910. By then, people in Colorado had started talking about Mrs. Decker as a candidate for the US Senate in 1912. Men as well as women agreed that they were ready to vote for her. As one newspaper said, "When Mrs. Decker takes hold there is something doing."[9] If she won, she would be the first woman to serve in either the United States House of Representatives or Senate—even before women could vote nationwide.

Sadly, there would be no Senator Decker. Just fifty-six years old, Sarah Platt Decker died of a sudden intestinal illness in July 1912.

Colorado's governor ordered that flags be flown at half-mast to show respect for Mrs. Decker. She was the first woman to lie in state at the Colorado State Capitol Building. Most state government offices closed on the day of her funeral as thousands turned out to mourn her. A former governor said, "She was the most popular and perhaps the greatest citizen of the state."[10]

Her tireless efforts had not only moved Colorado toward women's suffrage. Decker's leadership of the General Federation of Women's Clubs had resulted in an amazing list of progressive accomplishments by hundreds of thousands of clubwomen working together.

Unfortunately, those clubwomen failed many of their fellow women.

Most members of the GFWC were middle-class and upper-middle-class women. Like the population of the United States in the early twentieth century, they were also mostly white and Protestant (over three-fourths of Americans were white and Protestant during the early 1900s—today it's about one-third[11]). Other women's groups were the same. Those clubwomen were forward-thinking in many ways, but they also reflected the sometimes harmful attitudes and values they'd grown up with. The member clubs of the GFWC usually refused to admit Black women. They often rejected Catholic women and Jewish women as well. Not all members of these groups supported those decisions. But that was the reality of society in the early twentieth century—segregated by race, religion, and ethnicity. And nationwide organizations tended to give in to racial or ethnic or religious discrimination in order to keep their segregationist members from quitting.

Think about what they lost by being exclusive. What would have happened if these groups had broadened their views on race and religion the way they had broadened their view of women's work? They might have seen that women from minority or marginalized groups had many of the same concerns and hopes as white, Protestant women did. Minority women could be as progressive in their thinking as white women—sometimes more progressive. And Black women in particular had always had a wide view of the domestic sphere. These women shared a lot of the same values and could bring their own skills and experiences to the table. One of those values was coming together to solve problems.

Then, In-Between, and Now: Women's Clubs

Then: Most early women's clubs were social, literary, or church groups. But many of them shifted their focus to service and reform during the late 1880s. Hundreds of those clubs then came together as the General Federation of Women's Clubs in 1890.

Clubs worked on all sorts of projects across the country. But membership was usually limited to white, Protestant women (that changed gradually during the 1960s and '70s as individual state chapters opened their membership to all women). One exception was the Federation of Women's Clubs of Indian Territory—founded by clubwomen of Native American descent in Oklahoma. It became part of the GFWC in 1904.[12]

Black women could not join the GFWC. They formed their own local clubs and the National Association of Colored Women. The NACW worked for many of the same causes that the GFWC did, but it also lobbied for anti-lynching laws and fought discrimination.

Nannie H. Burroughs, president, National League of Republican Colored Women

The National Council of Jewish Women—formed in 1893—gave Jewish women a voice and offered them a way to make stronger connections to their faith and to Jewish history and culture. It also provided

Jewish women with opportunities to support social justice reform. Members worked for women's and children's rights, as well as anti-lynching laws.[13]

Officers of the National Council of Jewish Women, Atlanta section, 1910–1912

Fewer Catholic women came together in clubs. Those who did supported most of the same goals as other women's clubs. But many Catholic women were immigrants or the daughters of immigrants and wanted to protect their ethnic and religious traditions. Like Black middle-class women, they felt a responsibility to lift their people with them as they fought anti-Catholic discrimination and prejudice. They worked to prove that they could be Irish and Catholic, or Italian and Catholic, etc., and true Americans at the same time.

Often, Catholic women who didn't join clubs were already doing volunteer work through their parish churches and schools. Others chose a different way to serve. Rather than marrying and having children, they devoted their lives to service in religious communities as nuns or sisters. Tens of thousands of Catholic women in these communities ran hospitals, schools, orphanages, and more.

The majority of women's clubs did not work for women's suffrage the way other women's organizations did. But individual clubwomen like Sarah Platt Decker strongly supported the vote for women. Many of them came to believe that the vote was the only way to accomplish their goals and protect their many achievements.[14] Still, women's clubs' real purpose was reform—in housing, health care, city services, conservation, child welfare, and more.

In-Between: The popularity of women's clubs peaked in the mid-1920s, with some two million American women members. Economic hardship hurt membership during the 1930s. Then, during World War II, women of all classes took on factory jobs, military work, farmwork, and more. When they left those jobs after the war, they often wanted something beyond the domestic sphere. And by then they had more opportunity to attend college and enter professions. Many women no longer felt the need for clubs. They now made their social connections through school and work.

By the 1960s, middle-class women worked outside the home in greater numbers than ever before. They also took up political causes including civil rights and women's rights and were active in their communities. But they generally acted without joining traditional women's clubs.

In some areas, women's clubs shifted their focus (as they had in late 1800s) to meet the needs members saw around them. In the suburbs that popped up all over the country after World War II, women formed welcome clubs to help new neighbors adjust to a new way of life, though more narrow-minded women used these clubs to keep their neighborhoods "pure." Native American women's clubs fought for education that encouraged tribal children to learn mainstream American culture, but also Indigenous languages and culture. Tribal people had lost much of that heritage between the mid-1800s and the mid-1900s. A horrifying, misguided US government policy at that time had forced Indigenous children to become "Americanized" on reservations, at boarding schools, and through forced adoption. Black women lobbied for school desegregation and voting rights. Jewish women fought anti-Semitism. The list of causes goes on. But membership in traditional women's clubs continued to fall.

Now: Women's clubs today have opened their membership to people of all races, religions, and ethnic groups. Yet far fewer women belong to women's clubs now than during the early twentieth century. GFWC membership is currently about sixty thousand. That's less than 10 percent of what it was in 1920.[15] The NACW has fewer members today too.

Are women today less engaged in their communities than they were a hundred years ago? Do they simply have no time for service clubs? About 75 percent of women ages twenty-five to fifty-four were in the workforce as of 2023.[16] But there's more to declining club membership than time.

Many women in the twenty-first century participate

in organizations that didn't exist in 1920. For example, professional women often come together to support one another outside of clubs. They identify by profession rather than cause. And new technologies allow these women to connect across great distances rather than meet in their own neighborhoods. Plus, the work women did all those years ago has paid off. Women are now welcome to join civic and business organizations and clubs that used to be men-only. And thousands of women today are political and social activists but do not belong to clubs. They use their First Amendment rights to march, speak, and write for broad reproductive rights or against them, for LGBTQA+ rights or against them, for environmental issues, child welfare issues, and more. But membership in civic and cultural clubs has declined among both women and men in recent years.

And so: The numbers raise questions. Are Americans today less connected to their communities than they were years ago? Does modern technology allow them to be more aware of global issues than ever before, but less aware of their neighbors' needs? Does time spent at work mean that women and men have no time for volunteerism or social connection? If so, what does that mean for the country? For the American "principle of association"? For reaching out to one another to get things done? Has Americans' sense of community moved in new directions? Or is that sense of community dying? Will the pendulum swing back toward the principle of association? Can it?

CHAPTER 16

★★★

Other Voices

Mary Church Terrell—"Mollie" to her friends and family—had traveled to Berlin, Germany, for the 1904 meeting of the International Congress of Women. The ICW had held its first conference in Paris in 1878. Its goal was to bring women's groups from around the world together to discuss and join forces on issues including suffrage, education, professional opportunities, and more.

As one of the most educated women in the United States or anywhere else at the time, Terrell had been invited to speak at the Berlin conference on the status of Black American women. When the time came, Terrell stood before the international audience and delivered her address in English and then in perfect German (she later gave the speech again in French). Terrell could have used ancient Greek or Latin as well, if anyone would have understood her.

The audience erupted in a standing ovation. Women from dozens of countries and cultures applauded Terrell's language abilities as well as the content of her speech. One report said, "The eloquence of her words carried the audience by storm and she had to respond three times to the encores before they were

Mary Church Terrell, between 1880 and 1900

satisfied."[1] It wasn't the first time Mollie Terrell had impressed the people around her.

Robert and Louisa Church—Mollie's parents—were both born into slavery. Despite having no opportunity for education, they'd done very well after their emancipation with the small businesses they built in Memphis, Tennessee. But they wanted more for their daughter. They knew that Mollie had a very good mind, and they wanted her to make the most of it. Unfortunately, the one school for Black children in Memphis was crowded and poor. So as hard as it was, the Churches decided to send Mollie away at the age of eight to attend school in Ohio in 1871.[2] Imagine leaving home that young.

Mollie missed her family terribly, but she loved school and reminded herself of how lucky she was. For the rest of her life, Mollie Church believed in the value of education. She was certain that education was the key to finding good jobs. But she also knew it was much more than that. Education allowed people to develop their minds and spirits. And Mollie realized as she grew older that she had learned much more than academics during her school years. She had learned how to survive.

Church had both white and Black friends at school. Even so, she felt the reality of racial prejudice and discrimination. She felt the sting of many classmates' racism when they excluded her or told her she could not be both Black and pretty. Think of hearing that and having no one to turn to for reassurance and a hug. Incidents like that taught Mollie that the world could be a hard place for a girl like her. She was usually a rule follower, but she decided that she would not let those children treat her badly. She would physically fight them on the playground if she had to. And she would accept the consequences with her head high.[3] This was Mollie Church's awakening—at eight years old.

Church went on to Oberlin College in Ohio—the first US college to admit Black students (in 1835) and one of a very small number of US colleges that accepted Black students or women in the late 1800s. She took the four-year "men's course" at Oberlin rather than the less challenging, two-year "women's course."[4] Very few Oberlin women chose that route. But that was how Mollie was able to study Latin and Greek. Those subjects weren't in the women's course because most people, including some college officials and professors, believed that women weren't bright enough to learn ancient languages. They thought that even those who might be able to do the work would certainly never make use of that knowledge. Mollie didn't let that narrow thinking stop her for a minute.

Church excelled at Oberlin. She earned a bachelor of arts degree in 1884. Education would be her armor against racism and sexism. It would give her a path to move up in a society that worked to keep her down. She wished that for all Black Americans.

After graduation, Mollie moved home to Memphis, Tennessee, as her father wished. But Robert Church didn't want his daughter to take a job. He was a wealthy man, and no wealthy man's daughter worked outside the home and charitable causes. But a life of teas and socials wasn't for Mollie. She sounded a lot like Lillian Wald when she said, "I could not be happy leading a purposeless existence."[5]

Church left Memphis, took a teaching position at Wilberforce University in Ohio, and worked toward a master's degree at Oberlin. Then she moved to Washington, DC, for a job at a very prestigious academic high school. All of this flew in the face of American society's expectations for women. Especially Black women.

The M Street High School in Washington, DC, was one of the first high schools for Black children in the country. And it was more than that. The school stressed high-level academic work. Students at M Street learned mathematics and languages and literature. They prepared for college. That was what attracted Mollie Church.

M Street High School (Perry School)

Mollie saw an opportunity to give Black students the kind of education she had received in Ohio. A kind of education that was very rare for Black children in the United States. Mollie was impressed with the school and pleased with her students' progress during her first year there. Many of them went on to college and would become professionals—their lives transformed by education.

The following year, Mollie had the chance to further her own education in France and Germany. She left the M Street High School and went to Europe for two years. Life for Black Americans wasn't perfect in European countries. But it was much easier than life in the US. Church experienced less discrimination in Europe, less prejudice, fewer negative assumptions about her abilities, and more freedom to do what she wanted. That would be hard to give up, and she considered staying in Europe permanently.

In the end, though, Mollie Church couldn't abandon Black America. Like Lugenia Burns Hope in Atlanta, Mollie believed that educated, well-off Black Americans had a responsibility to pull all Black Americans up with them. People like Church and Hope had to show white society that stereotyped images of Black Americans—and the prejudices that went with them—were wrong. Mollie called it "lifting as we climb." And she couldn't do it from Europe. She wrote, "I knew I would be happier trying to promote the welfare of my race in my native land."[6]

Church returned to the United States and to the M Street High School. She also reconnected with Robert "Berto" Terrell, who'd been a fellow teacher at the school. Berto, born into slavery in 1857, had been the third Black graduate of Harvard University and the first to graduate with honors. Now he had a law degree from Howard University and a job at the US Department of the Treasury in Washington. He and Church married in 1891.

Mollie had hesitated to marry because it meant she would have to give up teaching. Married women were not permitted to teach in most schools across the country. She and Berto both thought that policy was ridiculous. It was one more reason that women needed equal rights with men. But there was nothing they could do. Mollie gave in because she loved Berto, but she had no intention of giving up her support for education or her determination to lift the Black community.

Robert Terrell was proud of his wife's commitment to racial and gender equality. However, it put the two of them in a difficult spot. While Robert was more than qualified for his job, he still had to be careful not to anger the white men he worked with, not to appear "uppity" or too sure of himself. As his wife, Mollie felt the same responsibility.

Yet she couldn't pretend to be less than she was. She just didn't have it in her. And Berto would never want her to. Mollie wasn't content to wait quietly for racial or gender equality to suddenly appear out of thin air. She wasn't going to wait for white women's clubs to invite Black women to join them. To wait for men to acknowledge women's abilities and rights. She wasn't willing to sit back and do nothing about injustice.

Washington, DC, had a fairly large Black middle class compared to a lot of American cities in the late 1800s. Middle-class Black women in Washington had formed a variety of clubs with a range of purposes—social, intellectual, charitable. Many were connected to churches. Mollie Church Terrell thought that those clubs could be more effective if they worked together the way white women's clubs were doing under the General Federation of Women's Clubs. She and several other prominent Black women invited the existing clubs to join a new Colored Women's League (CWL) in 1892.

The CWL's goals were very similar to the goals of other

women's service clubs—assisting children, women, and the poor. Members immediately started raising money for a kindergarten for Black children. They organized adult night classes and more. The CWL was soon the largest Black women's club in the United States.

That same year, the terrible reality of racism pushed Mollie toward wider and more forceful activism. A childhood friend, Thomas Moss, was lynched—murdered—in Memphis. Imagine the shock of learning that a friend had been violently, horribly murdered for no reason other than his race. Sadly, that kind of news was common in the Black community. A scuffle in a grocery store had grown into a white mob rampage. The mob pulled a dozen or more Black men, including Moss, from their homes and businesses and put them in jail for no reason.

During the night, the white mob came back to the jail and took Moss and two other men to a field. They shot the men multiple times and left their bodies lying on a railroad track.[7]

Mollie Terrell was heartbroken. So was Ida B. Wells, a Memphis journalist and close friend of Thomas Moss. Both women knew that no one would ever be arrested for these crimes. Nothing would be done. How could it be that the murder of a white person—even a person with a long criminal record—brought investigations and trials, while everyone ignored the murder of a Black person with no criminal record at all?

Independently, both women started anti-lynching efforts. Like other progressive journalists did for other issues, Wells used her skills to investigate lynchings. In Memphis, she printed a pamphlet exposing what she had learned and wrote an angry editorial for the *Free Speech*. She called lynching "an excuse to get rid of Negroes who were acquiring wealth and property and thus keep the race terrorized."[8]

Wells's words angered local white supremacists. They destroyed the printing press at the newspaper office and threatened Wells with death. Ida B. Wells left Memphis, but she devoted herself to informing people about the truth of lynching through her writing and countless speeches all over the country.

In the meantime, Mollie Terrell started working with Frederick Douglass—the famous abolitionist who had escaped slavery and was now an advisor to presidents. Terrell and Douglass invited Ida B. Wells to come to Washington and speak. Terrell also began making public speeches herself. But the lynching wasn't the only event that pushed her to action.

Soon after Thomas Moss's death, Mollie Terrell had become very ill while she was pregnant for the first time. She almost died of kidney failure. And sadly, she lost the baby. Mollie knew that things might have turned out differently if she had had access to the quality of medical care that white women did. Think of the pain of always wondering if the baby might have lived if she had been a white woman.

Terrell threw herself into the Black women's club movement. She began speaking on lynching, unequal health care, and more. And, still passionate about education, she accepted a seat on Washington, DC's board of education in 1895.

Mary Church Terrell was the first Black woman to hold a school board seat in any major city in the United States. She worked on behalf of all students but focused on the needs of Black children. She defended Black teachers who were unfairly accused of misconduct. And she succeeded in instituting a "Frederick Douglass Day" in the district's Black schools. Eventually that day became Negro History Week, a forerunner to the national Black History Month of today.

Terrell thought that her biggest success in education came when she convinced the DC board of education to eliminate

Mary Church Terrell House, Washington, DC

oral exams for students who wanted to enter "normal school," or teacher training.[9] In an oral exam, the applicant met with examiners in person to answer questions instead of taking a written exam. Mollie suspected that many Black applicants were rejected as soon as they walked into the exam room and the testing panel saw the color of their skin. Written exams would eliminate that element of discrimination and increase the number of well-qualified Black teachers.

While doing all that, Terrell also co-founded the National

Association of Colored Women (NACW). Similar to the GFWC, the NACW was the first non-religious Black association in the country. It became a base for political action. Members elected Mollie Terrell as their first president. They adopted her words, "Lifting as We Climb," as their motto.

Over time, Mollie had gained tremendous skill and confidence in her public speaking. She earned a strong reputation as she traveled across the country to deliver addresses to white as well as Black clubs and organizations. She was the only Black woman to give a speech at the 1898 National American Woman Suffrage Association (NAWSA) conference. Imagine how she must have felt when she received a standing ovation and several white women pushed their way through the crowd to hug her. That was unheard of at the time. It led to her 1904 speeches at the International Women's Congress in Berlin.

Mollie Terrell hadn't yet changed laws or eliminated racism. But her constant dignity, insistence on speaking the truth, and hard work was making a difference. And happily, after losing two more babies, Terrell gave birth to a healthy little girl.

In 1909, Mary Church Terrell went to New York to meet with other champions of equal rights. After an especially violent race riot in Illinois, a group of white reformers had organized a meeting to discuss racial justice. Many white progressives still believed in segregation or didn't want to cause trouble by opposing it. But fifty-three prominent white men and women answered the call and attended the meeting. Seven Black men and women, including Terrell, did the same. Together, they formed a new organization—the National Association for the Advancement of Colored People (NAACP). Their platform began, "We denounce the ever-growing oppression of our ten million colored fellow citizens as the greatest menace that threatens our country."[10]

Group portrait of men and women attending the NAACP-sponsored Amenia Conference in Amenia, New York, August 24–26, 1916

Mary Church Terrell was proud to sign the founding document. So was Ida B. Wells-Barnett (she had married some years earlier). Lillian Wald and Leonora O'Reilly were signers as well. The NAACP went to work against segregation and racism through lawsuits in the courts, lobbying lawmakers, educating the public, and more. Its work continues today.

Mollie Terrell went back to Washington and continued her work with various clubs. She never wavered in her determination to gain suffrage for American women. She picketed in front of the White House for women's voting rights in 1913, and put up with segregation and insults from white suffragists to participate in an enormous suffrage parade that year.

Terrell went on to demand equal rights for Black Americans throughout her long life. She always supported education as well. She co-founded the National Association of University Women (a Black women's group) and was the first Black member of the American Association of University Women. Both groups worked then and still work now to promote educational opportunities for women and youth and to advocate for women's issues.

All the while, the M Street High School stayed in Terrell's heart and mind. Under Principal Anna Julia Cooper, M Street students had outperformed white students on the city's academic tests. Many went on to prestigious colleges.

Head of suffrage parade in Washington, DC, March 3, 1913

Cooper, born into slavery just before the Civil War, was a classmate of Terrell's at Oberlin College and one of the most well-educated women—Black or white—in the country. She had worked her way through school and persisted through difficult times. She knew how much a good education had done for her and wanted that for every child. Especially Black children who would never have the kind of opportunities white children did. She believed in them, as the adults in her life had believed in her. If she could succeed after such humble beginnings, so could other Black children.

Anna Julia Cooper, principal, M Street High School, Washington, DC, 1902

But the success of the students at the M Street High School had bothered white school board members. When some of those students were admitted to Harvard and Yale Universities, it became ever more difficult for racists to insist that Black children were less intelligent than white children. Or that Black children were lazy. Their success proved every day that the members of the school board were wrong about Black children being capable of only job training and not real academic work. In 1906, the school board chose not to renew Anna Julia Cooper's contract as principal of the M Street School because she refused to use an inferior, less demanding "colored" curriculum.

Cooper went on to teach at and lead other educational institutions. She also raised her five nieces and nephews when their mother died. Eventually, she returned to teaching at the M Street High School and kept working, writing, and speaking for Black Americans' education. Mollie Terrell continued that effort as well.

Mary Church Terrell could be difficult on occasion. She was demanding and liked to be in charge. Depression sometimes gripped her, especially when she lost each of three babies. But she always found a way to recover through her work. She wrote, "Obliged to be interested in the troubles and trials of others, I had little time to think of my own aching heart."[11] That attitude and drive benefited her neighborhood, her community, and her country in a time when Black activists including Terrell, Cooper, Wells, and Hope faced the challenges of racism even within their own movements.

CHAPTER 17

★★★

The End of an Era

After years of hard work, a blizzard of progressive reform measures became law between 1900 and 1913. Progressives of every background and in every corner of the United States had persisted against all opposition. They had persevered against criticism and corruption. They had organized tens of thousands of volunteers. Written hundreds of thousands of letters and campaigned for candidates who supported their causes. They had succeeded in electing progressives to state offices and the presidency. And they had persuaded state legislatures and the US Congress to enact reform. Perhaps most significantly, they had widened Americans' idea of democracy and of government's role in American life.

Women like Albion Bacon and Leonora O'Reilly pressed states and the federal government to enact "social justice" laws—tenement and factory safety regulations, limits on child labor, protections for workers, and so on. Clubwomen like Sarah Platt Decker pushed for new federal bureaus that now oversaw conservation of natural resources, meat inspection, food and drug production, and more. Lillian Wald and Lugenia Burns Hope fought for better health care and community services for low-income and minority Americans. Mary Church Terrell pressed for better schools and educational opportunities for all children.

Many progressive women and men also worked to enlarge democracy through women's suffrage. And they looked for ways to make government less corrupt, more accountable, and responsible to all voters. They promoted changes that would give ordinary citizens a greater voice in their democracy.

All over the United States, progressives were ready to keep going as they welcomed the new year in 1914. Membership in women's clubs was growing (unfortunately, still mostly segregated by race and religion). Membership in the NAACP was increasing as well (though segregationist progressives weren't pleased with that). Progressive political candidates campaigned for an eight-hour workday, national health service, insurance for the elderly and disabled, insurance for injured workers, women's suffrage, and more.

However, two catastrophic events—a war and a pandemic—changed everything. Including the direction and priorities of the American people.

Tensions had been building in Europe for years. Why? A number of European nations—Great Britain, France, Germany, Russia, and others—were competing to enlarge their empires in Africa and Asia and began to build their individual military power. They increased the size of their armies and navies and stockpiled weapons. They and other nations also promoted very strong "nationalism." This nationalism was more than just a feeling of patriotism. It pushed people's national and ethnic pride into a feeling of superiority over other nations or cultures. National and ethnic pride also led some European ethnic groups to demand independence from the Austro-Hungarian and Ottoman Empires. It was a recipe for disaster.

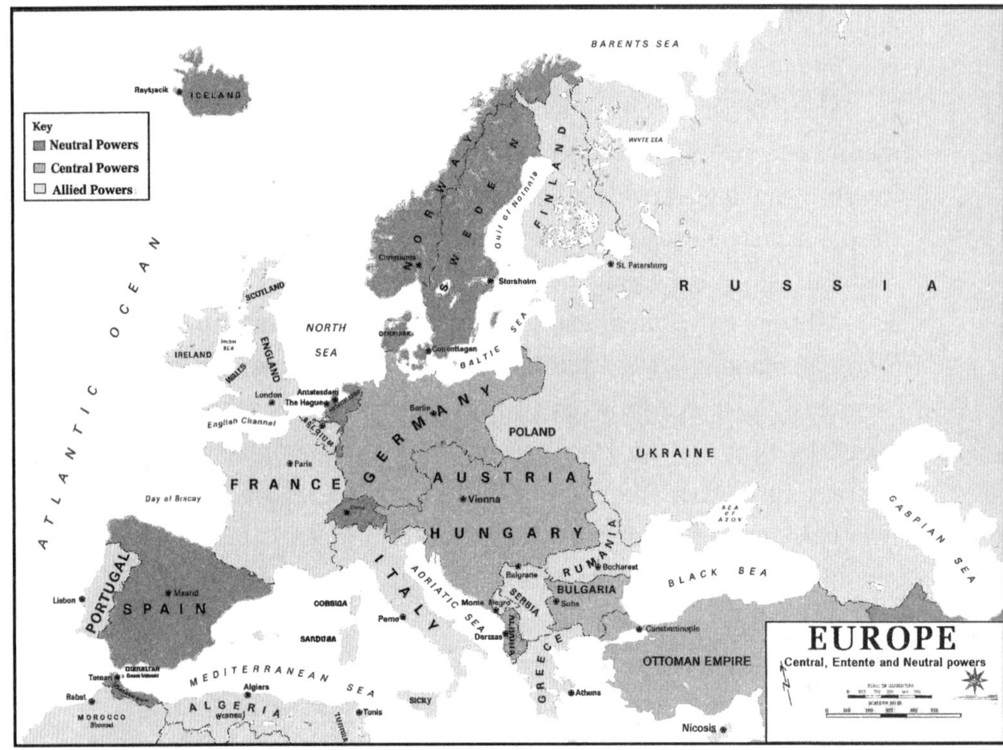

Europe in 1914

The majority of Americans didn't pay much attention to events in Europe. After all, Europe was an ocean away. Would anything that happened there affect the United States?

Yes, it would.

An organization of nationalist Serbs in Bosnia wanted independence from the Austro-Hungarian Empire, even if that meant violence. In June 1914, a member of that group assassinated Austria's Archduke Franz Ferdinand. Even Americans who didn't read the news had to see the enormous headlines everywhere. Most of them couldn't have found Bosnia or Serbia on a map, or said what an archduke was exactly. But a royal assassination sounded serious.

In late July, Austria-Hungary declared war on Serbia. Within a week, Germany declared war on Russia and France. Britain declared war on Germany. France declared war on Austria. Ordinary people could hardly keep track. How did any of it make sense?

Most people in the United States and in Europe were not aware that many European governments had joined secret alliances. Each member of an alliance promised to defend any other member in war. As a result, that first declaration of war pulled all the other countries into the conflict in a chain reaction.

Headlines piled one on top of another. The situation was mind-boggling even to the Europeans whose countries were part of it. In a matter of days, almost the entire European continent had gone to war.

The Great War—what we now call World War I—would drag on for four years and become the deadliest war in history to that point. No one knew that at the start, of course. Leaders made fiery speeches and citizens waved flags and vowed to fight the enemy. Young men rushed to join their country's military—they didn't want to miss out on the adventure they imagined war would be. And the whole thing would be over by Christmas, wouldn't it? Still, no one could really explain *why* they were going to war.

President Woodrow Wilson announced that the United States would remain neutral. The US would stay out of the conflict and not support either side. But that declaration of neutrality didn't change the way people thought. Some Americans supported Germany because they or their ancestors came from that country. Many Irish immigrants opposed Britain because Ireland was under British control and the Irish wanted independence (Irish and German immigrants were the largest immigrant groups in the US at the time). Many other Americans supported Great Britain because the US and Britain shared a culture, a language, and democratic ideals.

Many progressives opposed war in Europe or anywhere else. They believed that war would never solve problems. Fighting would only take attention and resources away from finding real solutions. Lillian Wald, Leonora O'Reilly, and Mary Church Terrell were among those who thought that way.

Just a few weeks after the conflict started, Lillian Wald helped organize the Women's Peace Parade in New York City. Over a thousand women walked solemnly along Fifth Avenue. Spectators lining the sidewalks watched in silence. The only sound was a quiet roll of drums. Wald went on to co-found the American Union Against Militarism. About six thousand people had joined by 1915.[1]

Women's Peace Party's parade, New York City, August 1915

As the war continued into 1916, some Americans volunteered to fight with the French Foreign Legion. A small number became pilots for France or Britain. And others, including several thousand Indigenous Americans, joined the Canadian forces going to support the British. Many progressive women—whether they supported Britain or Germany or neither—shifted their attention to helping the innocent victims of the fighting.

The American Red Cross—founded in 1881 by Civil War nurse Clara Barton—enlisted hundreds and then thousands of women to aid the victims of the Great War. Some became ambulance drivers (very few women had driver's licenses at the time). Professionally trained women served as nurses and doctors in England, France, Serbia, and Russia. They often risked their lives to treat the wounded. Some actually gave first aid in the trenches as the battle raged around them. Others worked in overwhelming conditions at field hospitals. Chief Nurse Julia Stimson described a nurse who was sick to her stomach from the smell in the operating room.

> She . . . kept right on with her work . . . sewing and tying up and putting in drains while the doctor takes the next piece of shell out of another place. Then after fourteen hours of this, with freezing feet, to a meal of tea and bread and jam, and off to rest if you can in a wet bell tent in a damp bed without sheets after a wash with a cupful of water. . . . One need never tell me that women can't do as much, stand as much, and be as brave as men.[2]

Some women of privilege, including Anne Morgan—daughter of finance tycoon J. P. Morgan—organized relief efforts of their own. Morgan was an outspoken progressive who supported women's suffrage and walked picket lines with garment workers and others. She owned a house in France with two other women. Soon after the war began, they turned the house into a hospital for wounded soldiers.

Poster of a Red Cross nurse holding wounded US soldier on stretcher

Morgan then turned to the thousands of ordinary French farm families and villagers who had lost their homes to artillery fire and bombs. She had visited the "front"—the area where the fighting went on. No amount of money or privilege could protect her there, but she wanted to find out what was happening. Picture what she saw. Farm fields destroyed by bombs. Houses reduced to rubble. People who had nothing left. Nothing.

Morgan took action. She organized the American Committee for Devastated France and began gathering data on families' needs. By the end of the war, Morgan and her partners had provided millions of dollars in food relief. She and the nurses and others who joined her worked right in the midst of the destruction. They repaired houses or found new housing for over fifty thousand French people. They built clinics, homes for orphaned children, and schools. They brought in livestock and seed and farm equipment to help farmers get started again.[3]

In 1918, the French military awarded Morgan and her partner Anne Murray Dike the French Croix de Guerre (Cross of War), an honor given for acts of bravery.[4] That award could have gone to every nurse, doctor, and aid worker in the country.

Meanwhile, US neutrality had ended when Germany began submarine attacks on American cargo ships in 1917. The United States declared war on Germany in April of that year. Suddenly, the ocean between the US and Europe didn't seem nearly wide enough.

Tens of thousands of American soldiers boarded ships for Europe. Tons of equipment, arms, munitions, and food crossed the Atlantic as well. Thousands of women went into jobs that men had held before. Other thousands waited and worried as their loved ones volunteered or were drafted into the military.

✣✣✣

US Army (doughboy army) in France, 1918

By the time the war ended in 1918, over twenty million people (military and civilian) had died. The United States reported about 117,000 military deaths and close to 1,000 civilian deaths. France suffered nearly two million military and civilian deaths. Russia lost even more of its people. And in the areas where most of the fighting had occurred, additional millions of men, women, and children were wounded or starving or homeless. The world had never seen anything like it.

Before anyone could take a deep breath, however, an even more deadly enemy appeared—disease.

American soldiers returned to flag-waving crowds and parades in 1918 and 1919. Unknowingly, they brought a particularly contagious strain of influenza (flu) with them. Soldiers going home to other countries did the same. The first cases appeared at military bases. Within months, people all over the US and around the world were falling ill and dying. In crowded cities, small towns, farmlands, and remote areas, whole families became infected. No one had a treatment for the disease. One woman in Boston lost her husband and five of her six children in less than a week. Tragedies like that happened everywhere.

Victims felt fine one minute, and then suddenly feverish. Within hours, they were choking as fluid filled their lungs and closed off their breathing. The majority of victims recovered. But thousands didn't. The elderly and small children died in large numbers, as often happens with diseases like influenza. But younger adults also died at surprisingly high rates—something medical experts couldn't explain.

Emergency hospital at Brookline, Massachusetts, to care for influenza cases

Lillian Wald led the fight to save lives in New York City. She had the medical and organizational skills to take on the enormous task. As one biographer described it:

> Amid the tremendous suffering of that epidemic, she slept very little, caring for patients and nurses, enlisting volunteers for the work, and appealing to benefactors to fund it.[5]

Despite efforts like Wald's and others, 25 percent of Americans—one in every four people in the United States—caught influenza in just one year. Nearly seven hundred thousand Americans died—six times the number of Americans who had died in the war. It was about one-half of 1 percent of the population at that time (by comparison, the US lost 1.2 million people to COVID-19 between 2020 and 2022—about one-sixth of 1 percent of the population[6]). Experts estimate that one-third of all the people in the world became infected with influenza. At least fifty million people died.[7]

Influenza faded away in late 1919. No one knew how or why at the time (we now know that that strain of influenza didn't die out, but weakened and became the seasonal flu we still face today). Imagine the exhaustion people must have felt after years of war and disease.

Americans entered the new decade of the 1920s hoping for calm. Hoping that life could go back to the way it used to be before the Great War—or at least the way they *imagined* it had been. But their mood had changed from what it was before. So had their priorities. Reform and demand for change seemed exhausting to people worn out by worry and sorrow. After three progressive presidents in a row, conservative Republican presidential candidate Warren G. Harding called for lower taxes, limits on immigration, and "a return to normalcy" in 1920. Exactly what many Americans yearned for. He won the election easily.

What would that mean for progressives?

Then, In-Between, and Now: The People's Political Power

Then: Voting is the greatest political power an ordinary citizen has. But only white males over the age of twenty-one could vote in most places at the start of the Progressive Era. A number of progressives worked to change that. Many supported women's suffrage. Some fought for suffrage for Black Americans, though the majority of people who thought of themselves as progressives did not. Progress was very slow.

Progressive men and women had more success in finding ways to make government less corrupt and more accountable and responsible to all voters. And they pushed to give ordinary citizens a greater voice.

Many cities and towns at the time filled jobs and made policies based on bribery and favoritism (though they didn't say so). Progressives promoted more professional ways of operating. As a result, most US cities and towns reformed their governments. They adopted either:

- a council-manager system in which elected council members appoint a professional city manager to oversee departments and carry out policy, or
- a mayor-council system with an elected mayor and elected city council, each with specific powers.

Both systems rely on skills and knowledge rather than bribery and favoritism. Both give voters more power. Most American cities and towns still use these systems.

Progressives also worked for more voter power at the state level. Many states responded by instituting:

- primary elections where voters choose the member of their political party who will run for office,
- the initiative, which allows the public to petition to put a proposed law on the ballot at election time,
- the referendum, giving voters the power to accept or reject a law that the state legislature has passed, and
- recall, providing a way for voters to remove a public official from office before his or her term has ended.

Progressive reformers also pushed for "amendments"—changes—to the US Constitution itself. But amending the Constitution isn't easy. The framers wanted change to be possible, but not too quick and easy. That could result in changes based on momentary wishes rather than carefully considered proposals. So the path to amending the Constitution requires approval from two-thirds of the House of Representatives and two-thirds of the US Senate. Then the measure must have approval from three-fourths of the states for "ratification"—final approval. Since 1789, the Constitution has been amended only twenty-seven times, including the ten amendments of the Bill of Rights. As of 2024, no amendment has been ratified for over forty years.

Despite the challenge, the Sixteenth Amendment became part of the Constitution in 1913. It gave the federal government the power to collect a tax on income from every American who made money. This allowed the federal government to pay for the National Park Service, the US Forest Service, meat inspectors, and so on. And wealthy Americans would pay a greater percentage of their income in federal income tax, since they could easily afford it.

That same year, the Seventeenth Amendment changed the way US senators were chosen. Instead of state legislatures choosing those who would serve as senators in Washington, voters would elect their state's senators.

In-Between: The struggle for voting rights and political power didn't end with Progressive Era reforms. Women finally won the right to vote with the Nineteenth Amendment in 1920, just as the era was ending. But most American men and women of color were still locked out of voting by state laws and intimidation, especially in the South. Fortunately, reformers or activists continued the work, and more American people gradually gained political power.

- Women began to win elected offices during the 1920s and '30s, though it was slow going. By 1990, just thirty-one of 535 seats in the US Congress were held by women (in 2024 that number was 150 of 535).
- Women were appointed to more government offices than ever before during the '20s and '30s.
- The Voting Rights Act of 1965 gave Black Americans protection against the tactics (such as literacy tests, taxes, and terror) that had kept them from voting. At the time, 30 percent more white citizens were registered to vote than Black citizens. By 1975, that difference had dropped to 8 percent.[8]

- The Twenty-Sixth Amendment (1971) lowered the voting age to eighteen. Young men being drafted into the military would now be able to vote for the lawmakers who could pass draft laws.
- The Equal Rights Amendment ("Equality of rights under the law shall not be denied or abridged by the United States or by any State on account of sex" had been introduced in Congress for the first time in 1923. In 1972, it finally passed in both houses of Congress and went to the states for ratification. A dispute over whether the amendment has met the requirements to become part of the Constitution continues as of 2024.

Now: American democracy has expanded to include more women and minorities than in the past. At the federal level in 2024:

- women made up about 25 percent of Congress and about 40 percent of federal judges and Supreme Court justices,
- people of color made up about 29 percent of Congress,
- thirteen members of Congress were openly gay, lesbian, or bisexual,
- Sarah McBride was the first transgender person elected to Congress, and
- half of President Joe Biden's cabinet members were women; half of all members were people of color.

At the state and local level, more women and minorities were in positions of leadership. And the reforms of the

Progressive Era—primary elections, referendums, direct election of senators, etc., remained in place.

Even so, many Americans today worry that their voices and their political power are in danger. Why?

Laws passed during the late twentieth century regulated the money that went into political campaigns. The goal was to avoid the corruption of making political donations to gain favors. But a 2010 Supreme Court ruling overturned much of that regulation as violating free speech. Businesses and billionaires can now put as much money as they want into a candidate's campaign. And candidates do not have to tell the public who they are taking money from—very similar to the Gilded Age. These changes led to many questions, including:

- Is money free speech?
- Will candidates who quietly accept millions of dollars from one person or one industry act on the promises they make to voters, or set aside their promises and work just for their big donors?
- How do ordinary citizens compete with billionaires to support their candidates?

In 2013, the Supreme Court ruled that parts of the 1965 Voting Rights Act were unconstitutional. Several states soon passed laws making it more difficult for many low-income citizens and people of color to vote. In those states, the gap between white and Black voter turnout has increased after decreasing for years.[9]

Today's activists question what all this means for the future of Progressive Era achievements. They question what it means for representative democracy.

CHAPTER 18

★★★

Legacy

No one announced the end of the Progressive Era in 1920. There's no way to know exactly when an era or a movement begins or ends. Time would tell. But progressives, like the tycoons of the Gilded Age, had to wonder if the party was over. And many historians consider Warren G. Harding's election the end of the Progressive Era.

Warren G. Harding, 1920

Harding and the two Republican presidents who followed him believed that the country needed to return to a more laissez-faire government. They thought that if big business did well, everyone would benefit. Calvin Coolidge said, "The chief business of the American people is business."[1] He didn't mean that *only* business mattered. Or that the American people shouldn't look out for one another. But he and the others did believe that business was the key to a stable nation. They maintained that tax laws that favored business, as well as fewer business regulations, would keep the economy strong. Just as many politicians of the Gilded Age did (and many do today).

Calvin Coolidge, around 1924

Did that mean that all the work Wald, Bacon, Hope, O'Reilly, Decker, Terrell, and thousands of other progressive women had done was going to be undone?

The 1920s did see less government concern for workers' and consumers' safety. For example, experts pointed out the deadly dangers of lead in gasoline in 1922. But the government ran no tests and allowed leaded gasoline to be sold to the public for decades after the discovery.[2] That same year, young women who painted illuminated dials on watches started dying. Radium in the paint they used was causing cancer and radium poisoning. Manufacturers knew this, but hundreds or even thousands of women died before the government stepped in.[3]

At the same time, conservation supporters saw national forests and federal lands opened to mining, drilling, and timbering without regulation. And the child protections that progressives had championed suffered a blow when the Supreme Court ruled that only states and not the federal government could regulate child labor.

Progressives had good reason to be discouraged during the 1920s. But it seemed that no one told Lillian Wald or many others to feel that way. No one told them that the Progressive Era was over. Perhaps they were just too busy to hear the news.

Henry Street Settlement, 2011

Wald kept expanding the Henry Street Settlement through the 1920s and into the '30s. The settlement added training and arts programs. It established centers in more areas of New York City. And its workers reached more and more people—young and old, Black, white, and Asian, immigrants and native-born Americans. Lillian Wald retired in 1933 and died in 1940, but her work went on. Eventually, the nursing service became the Visiting Nurse Service of New York and expanded its care. Called VNS Health today, it is one of the largest not-for-profit health care organizations in the US. And the Henry Street Settlement now serves over fifty thousand New Yorkers every year in eighteen different locations.

✣✣✣

Albion Bacon didn't get the message about the end of the Progressive Era either. She could have retired from reform work after her Indiana housing bill success. Instead, Bacon turned to issues including juvenile courts and child labor. She chaired Indiana's child-welfare committee during the Great War. The committee gathered data on babies and young children to find ways to improve their health. When the war ended, Indiana's governor asked Bacon to be part of a new Commission on Child Welfare and Social Insurance. She accepted and helped to enact several state laws protecting children.

Herbert Hoover, between 1912 and 1930

Albion cut back on her speeches and travel as she entered her sixties. But she continued to push for reform programs in Evansville—the place where she had started her work. In 1931, President Herbert Hoover held a President's Conference on Home Building and Home Ownership.[4] Organizers established a number of committees to study all aspects of housing in the United States. They invited eleven of the nation's leading experts on housing regulations to sit on the Committee on Standards and Objectives. Albion Bacon was one of them. Her health was declining by then and she felt exhausted at the very idea of traveling back and forth to Washington, DC, for meetings. But she accepted. Bacon answered the call to serve others one more time.[5] She died in 1940.

✣✣✣

Lugenia Burns Hope led the NAACP in Atlanta long after 1920. She also continued as president of the Neighborhood Union in Atlanta for another two decades. The organization had gained a reputation around the country. Hope was in demand as a speaker for clubs and other groups who hadn't given up on progressive ideas any more than she had. She traveled all over, giving speeches and presentations about her work. Her methods for organizing a community, gathering data, and empowering local residents became an example for the reformers and activists she talked to.

Lugenia Burns Hope died in 1947. But the Neighborhood Union continued its work. Her model of community organizing became an early step in the modern civil rights movement of the 1950s and 1960s. Community organizing is still used today by groups supporting various causes and by both major political parties. In fact, Barack Obama started his political career as a community organizer.

Progressives could look back at their accomplishments with a lot of pride. But the movement was far from perfect—just as human beings are far from perfect. Progressives made mistakes. And some of what they did had unintended consequences—results that no one predicted.

The best example of that may be Prohibition—a national ban on alcoholic beverages. The movement to ban alcohol, known then as the temperance movement, had started in the 1820s. By about 1900, the push to promote temperance, or moderation in drinking, became a demand for total abstinence and laws against producing alcohol. Some progressives became very active in the movement. Other progressives opposed the ban. It seemed to step on people's liberties and private lives. But enthusiasm for prohibition grew, especially in rural areas. Supporters hoped that banning alcohol would save American families from the terrible and widespread consequences of alcohol abuse. The Eighteenth Amendment was ratified in 1919.

Young Barack Obama as community organizer in Chicago, Illinois

The ban did reduce alcohol consumption and the diseases alcohol causes. But Prohibition also created serious, unforeseen problems. Americans resented the ban. After all, not everyone who drank a little now and then abused alcohol. When they couldn't buy liquor legally, some turned to illegal sources. Organized crime—run by men like Al Capone—made fortunes selling illegal alcohol. Crime rings terrorized business owners in cities across the country. Deadly battles erupted between gangs. Police were overwhelmed by the violence in many cities. And

Prohibition agents pour liquor into sewer

thousands of ordinary people died or were blinded from drinking illegal "bootleg" whiskey that was poorly distilled or contained toxic ingredients.

By 1930, it was clear that the ban on alcohol had backfired. In 1933, the Twenty-First Amendment repealed the Eighteenth Amendment (the only time an amendment has been repealed), and alcohol became legal again. It remains legal, though alcohol consumption is linked to thousands of deaths in auto accidents and thousands more homicides every year.[6]

There were other kinds of mistakes or weaknesses in the progressive movement as well. Many white progressives supported the ugly racism, religious prejudice, and anti-immigrant, anti-newcomer feelings that swept the country at the time. They saw no conflict in being a progressive when it came to improving their own communities but a white supremacist when it came to the way they treated people who didn't look like them. Sadly, many other white progressives chose not to fight these prejudices. They looked the other way rather than lose support for their causes.

Similarly, white, middle-class, Protestant progressives often defined what it meant to be an American very narrowly. *They* were good Americans, but people from eastern Europe or Asia? Catholic or Jewish citizens? Maybe not. They assumed that immigrant, Catholic, Jewish, and Black cultures were inferior to their own—the only culture they believed was truly American. That attitude was common then (and still is in some places today), but that didn't make it factually correct or fair to millions of Americans from other backgrounds. Narrow thinking seeped into all sorts of progressive projects, from choosing what books to put in libraries to teaching cooking classes to improving public education.

So, did the mistakes progressives made or the weaknesses they showed outweigh their accomplishments? Was all the hard work, all the time, all the effort worth anything?

By 1920, the United States had far more parks and far more libraries than ever before. There were far fewer sweatshops and industrial accidents, and far less child labor than thirty years earlier. Most tenements had windows, as well as indoor toilets and hot running water. Canned and packaged food was safer to eat, and cases of food poisoning and typhoid fever had decreased. Twenty percent of children completed high school each year rather than the 5 percent who graduated in 1900.[7] The list of positive outcomes could go on and on. They don't excuse misguided prejudices, but they were remarkable achievements.

Even with all this new regulation—as well as new taxes—industrialists, landlords, and others continued to make millions. Mrs. Astor had died in 1908, and her son went down with the *Titanic* in 1912. But her four daughters, and the sons and daughters of other elite "old money" millionaires, married wealthy people and raised wealthy children of their own. So did the children of "new money" millionaires. Progressive ideas and policies in economics and government had not harmed them financially.

Perhaps the most important outcome of the Progressive Era, though—with its women reformers leading the way—was the "precedent," the model progressives set for making change.

Despite challenging times and their own failings, progressives didn't give up on the issues that were important to them. "Never frown, never sigh," as Sarah Platt Decker would say. They paved the way for an active government and continued the work even when the politics and mood of the country didn't want that during the 1920s. They proved the power of persuasion and persistence. And they remained convinced that government had a big role to play in promoting the common good. The Progressive Era might have ended. But progressivism had not.

When the Roaring Twenties crashed in 1929, the Great Depression of the 1930s blanketed the United States in hardship and hunger. No economic depression had ever been so bad. Millions of Americans found themselves out of work, without homes, and desperate.

In 1932, Americans rejected the laissez-faire leanings of the 1920s and elected Democrat Franklin Roosevelt in an enormous landslide. Some of the reformers who had been quite young during the Progressive Era now became part of Roosevelt's administration. They brought their expertise and determination with them.

The federal government became more active under Franklin Roosevelt (Theodore Roosevelt's distant cousin) than it had ever been before. The programs known as the New Deal put millions of Americans to work, created safety nets such as Social Security, protected workers and unions, regulated banking and the stock market, and more. The government continued to take an active role in the economy and society into the 1940s and 1950s as the country worked to survive and win World War II, and then move forward.

Franklin D. Roosevelt during a radio broadcast, 1933

Mary (Mollie) Church Terrell was there to see it all. Her passions for equality and education, and her pride in helping to establish the NAACP, came together in the early 1950s. More than forty years after co-founding the NAACP, Mollie Terrell filed a lawsuit against a restaurant in Washington, DC, that refused to serve her. She was eighty-six years old. The case went all the way to the Supreme Court, which ruled in her favor in 1953. Segregated eating facilities violated the US Constitution, the justices said. That ruling applied to restaurants and stores across the District of Columbia (the Civil Rights Act of 1964 would ban discrimination in public facilities nationwide). Terrell went back to the restaurant she had sued and was treated with dignity and respect. At the age of eighty-nine, Terrell saw

Portrait of Mary Church Terrell by Betsy Graves Reyneau, 1946

the change that she and so many others had worked for finally becoming reality.

That same year, NAACP attorney Thurgood Marshall (later the first Black justice of the Supreme Court) presented arguments before the Supreme Court in the case of *Brown v. Board of Education*. Mollie Terrell lived just long enough to hear the court's ruling declaring that racial segregation in public schools harmed children and was unconstitutional. Terrell, who died two months later at the age of ninety, knew that real, full integration was still a long way off. Protections and good education for all children were a long way off too. So was health care and decent housing and so much more. But she now had proof that persuasion and persistence could transform the nation. Mary Church Terrell would be remembered as a leader in that transformation. And her dedication, diligence, and persistence set an example for reformers going forward.

Like the women and men of the Progressive Era, later reformers understood that once progress is made, it must be protected. Defended against those who would tear it down or reverse it. Guarded against sliding backward. They knew then, and know today, that without dedication and diligence, reforms can slip away.

CHAPTER 19

★★★

New Voices, New Challenges

The Progressive Era can be seen as part of a pendulum's arc or the path of a backyard swing. The country moves toward government involvement and regulation for a while. Then it swings back toward small government and laissez-faire policies. Eventually, though, it moves toward progressivism again, then away from it, and so on.

But the swing toward reform at the turn of the twentieth century went further than many earlier reform movements had. And while the shift following Harding's election swung back, it didn't go *all* the way back to the 1890s—the Gilded Age, when a few very wealthy men controlled the government and economy. Progressives had made changes that felt permanent. Almost no one wanted to reverse food and drug safety laws or the direct election of senators. Americans liked most progressive reforms. But reforms were only part of what progressives did.

Leaders of the Progressive Era recognized that the rapid growth of new industries had remade the way people worked and lived. Those changes had caused many of the problems that made reform necessary. Individuals like Lillian Wald and Albion Bacon jumped in to find solutions. They looked for support from communities of volunteers, benefactors, and other reformers. And they concluded that they needed government support to make a lasting difference. This was a new way of thinking.

Industrialists like Rockefeller and Carnegie talked a lot about individualism—something Americans had always valued. But community had always been part of American life too. Remember Alexis de Tocqueville and his description of American "associations." Of everyday citizens connecting with one another to improve their communities.

Progressives added government to that idea of community. The American people came to agree with them. They agreed that their political leaders had a responsibility to the entire American community. A responsibility to "promote the general welfare," just as the US Constitution said.

In a time of bitter division, progressives found a way forward. They forged a middle path. On one side were the Gilded Age millionaires who wanted to continue their version of laissez-faire government. On the other side were the labor leaders and workers who believed they had to completely remake the American system of government and economics. The progressive middle path modified, reformed, and expanded American democracy by widening the idea of government's role. Without overthrowing it. Without violence. And within the law.

The United States is in another time of bitter division today. The country faces many of the same issues that it did during the Progressive Era—a huge wealth gap, a struggling working class, a few billionaires with enormous political power, and more.

Are there progressive reformers and activists today who can find a path forward despite these divisions?

Think of the characteristics progressives shared in the late 1800s. They were persuasive and persistent. They refused to give up even when reform was too slow to see. Remarkable progressive women didn't wait for anyone else to take action. When they saw a problem, they looked for a solution and learned what they needed to know to make a difference. Progressive presidents and administrations made reform easier to achieve. But these reformers pressed on with or without a president's support. They believed in American democracy and its possibilities.

The ability to act in the face of huge challenges hasn't changed, though the challenges may be greater than ever before. "Never frown, never sigh, keep step." Progressive activists across the country are following that advice right now, tackling the problems they see and building communities to solve those problems.

Lisa David spent thirty years working in public health. As of 2025, she leads Public Health Solutions, New York City's largest public health nonprofit. PHS provides health services to low-income and high-risk New Yorkers. PHS also conducts major research to assist New York's health department in making good decisions.[1]

Colonel Nicole Maan became the first Indigenous American woman to go into space when she commanded a NASA mission to the International Space Station in 2022. Maan is a graduate of the US Naval Academy, with a master's degree in mechanical engineering from Stanford University. She became a US Navy fighter pilot in 2002 and flew nearly fifty combat missions in Iraq and Afghanistan. NASA chose her for astronaut training in 2013.

Colonel Maan grew up in California. She has both European (Estonian) and Wailaki (Native American) ancestors. She is a member of the Round Valley Indian Tribe—a group of northern California Native American tribes. She often visits schools to inspire young people to follow their dreams no matter what barriers they face. She has reached out to Indigenous children in particular and did a livestream from space. "I brought a dreamcatcher from my mother that helped me through tough times as a child," she told them.[2]

As of early 2026, Mann is training for NASA's Artemis program, an international mission to land humans on the moon for the first time since 1972.

Alice Wong was born with a condition that causes muscles to weaken over time. She lost the ability to walk by the age of eight and used a motorized wheelchair and a device to help her breathe. Wong was the only physically disabled student at her school in Indiana, and one of very few Asian American students. As a child, she longed to be like the other children. But she had an awakening in her twenties. Wong decided that she wanted to be seen for her entire self, not just for her physical differences. And she vowed to gain greater access to public places for herself and other people like her. So, she studied disability history and medical sociology. Alice Wong then worked as an advocate for those with special needs. She fought for and won a variety of accommodations on her university campus for wheelchair accessibility, and for the hearing impaired and others. Wong served on the National Council on Disability and continued to work for both the disability community and for Asian Americans[3] until her death at the age of fifty-one in 2025.

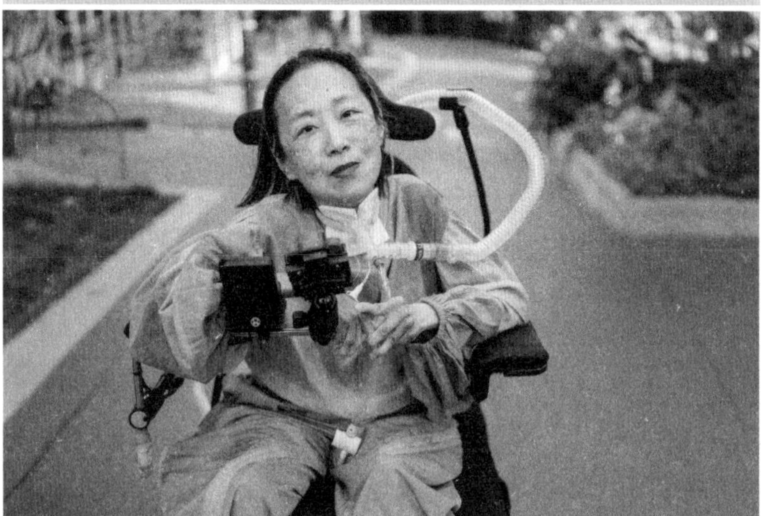

President Barack Obama hugs Mari Copeny (eight years old) backstage at Northwestern High School in Flint, Michigan, May 4, 2016

Mari Copeny was born in Flint, Michigan, in 2007. She was seven years old when the Environmental Protection Agency found that her city's water supply had high levels of lead. Lead poisoning in children can lead to delays in their development. It can result in learning difficulties, weight loss, hearing loss, seizures, and even death. Michigan's governor declared a state of emergency in Flint. Soon after, Mari wrote a letter to President Barack Obama. She asked him to meet with residents of Flint who were coming to Washington, DC, for congressional hearings on the crisis. The president answered that he would visit Flint. That visit put the situation in the national spotlight. And Obama authorized over $100 million to help correct the problem. During the emergency, the state of Michigan provided bottled water to people in Flint. That stopped in 2018, though the water was still not safe. Many of those people lived in low-income areas and could not afford to buy bottled water. So Mari began fundraising. The eleven-year-old raised nearly $300,000 to supply more than one million bottles of water to people in need. She then worked with a business to get water filters to Flint. As of 2025, Mari Copeny—a teenager—has continued to raise awareness and money to support the children of Flint. She has also served as a youth ambassador to environmental and women's organizations.[4]

Ani Zonneveld was born in Malaysia. Her father was a diplomat, and she grew up around the world. After college, she moved to Los Angeles to pursue a career in pop music. Ani was the first Malaysian artist to win a Grammy. After the events of September 11, 2001, Zonneveld started writing more spiritual music. She is a progressive Muslim and wanted to spread awareness of Islam as a religion of peace. In 2007, she founded Muslims for Progressive Values (MPV). The nonprofit group creates communities that welcome all people and promotes values of inclusion. Today MPV has chapters in North America, Europe, South America, and Malaysia. It offers programs focused on women's rights, interfaith families, and more. She is the author of *An Unlikely Social Justice Warrior: My Life as a Muslim Feminist.*[5]

Andrea Vidaurre was named one of the world's most influential people of 2025 by *Time* magazine, at the age of twenty-nine. Vidaurre grew up in an area of California known as the Inland Empire. Its location east of Los Angeles, as well as its relatively low-cost land and easy access to rail lines and highways, attracts many people who commute into Los Angeles or San Diego for work. Major businesses have built warehouses and distribution centers there as well. The result is massive traffic congestion that combines with California's climate to produce the worst air pollution in the United States. As a result, the area's mostly Latino, working-class communities where Vidaurre grew up experience very high death rates from asthma and other respiratory illnesses. Vidaurre is working to change that. She co-founded the People's Collective for Environmental Justice. Andrea Vidaurre and her colleagues succeeded in convincing the California Air Resources Board to adopt historic regulations on rail and trucking emissions. The collective continues to fight for zero emissions by 2036.[6]

These women, as well as thousands of other reformers, continue their efforts no matter which way the pendulum swings. But today's political divisions present new challenges.

CHAPTER 20

A Swing Too Far?

Think about the political pendulum. How far will it swing? A group of progressives at one end, which includes Alexandria Ocasio-Cortez and Bernie Sanders, support democratic socialism. They want to protect the principles of the US Constitution. They also want to protect private businesses. And they support much stronger regulations on big corporations, banks, and industry. They also support more government programs such as free health care for all.

A group of extreme conservatives at the other end of the political pendulum want a much smaller federal government. They want to eliminate business regulations. They also want to move many federal responsibilities—such as medical research, weather forecasting, and space exploration—to states or private businesses.

These differences are very similar to the differences of the Progressive Era. It should be up to voters to decide which way to swing—toward more government? Or toward laissez-faire policies?

Extreme conservatives (ultraconservatives) want more than laissez-faire policies. They want a president without checks and balances and with nearly unlimited power. A president who can act without Congress or the courts (or the people). Who can act outside the law.

This is the real challenge for progressives and for American democracy. Why? Most legal and constitutional experts agree that such unlimited presidential power violates the US Constitution. It goes against the principles of democracy.

We the People

Article 1

US Constitution

The United States Constitution sets up a representative democracy, also known as a constitutional republic. Many other nations also have representative democracies where citizens elect people to run the government for them. These governments can be organized in several ways, but they all share certain principles. In the US, these principles are spelled out in a written constitution.

- Respect for all people's rights
  - freedom of religion and speech
  - freedom to ask the government for change (petition) and come together to express opinions (assembly)

- Respect for the rule of law and due process
  - the law is the same for everyone — government leaders, police, military, citizens, and noncitizens
  - all government agencies and departments must follow the law
  - every person is treated fairly with the principle of "innocent until proven guilty" and a chance to defend themselves in court
  - the existence of a judicial branch where judges decide what is or isn't constitutional without political pressure or fear

- Limits on the power of the government and elected officials
  - each branch of government (legislative, executive, and judicial) has its own duties and powers
  - each branch of government has ways to check the power of the other two branches

- Free and fair elections
  - multiple political parties are allowed

- all adult citizens are allowed to vote
- elections are run fairly
- everyone is committed to accepting election results peacefully

- A free press (media)
  - media is able to criticize officials, expose corruption and abuse of power, hold officials accountable for their actions, and inform the public

Representative democracy is very strong. It's also very fragile. The American republic has faced attacks from foreign countries, a terrible civil war, and economic depressions. It has survived civil unrest, pandemics, and assassinations. It has overcome corruption and threats of revolution within the country.

In each crisis, the American people have stepped up to meet the challenge. Leaders and ordinary citizens from every political party have defended the Constitution. They have *made* the system work. When they disagree with election outcomes, court rulings, or executive policies, they use their constitutional rights and power to push for change, just as progressives did in the late 1800s. That's how democracy works.

But what will happen if one branch of government violates these principles? Ignores the Constitution and the law? What if people are arrested, jailed, or sent out of the country without due process? What if a president rejects court orders? Or threatens judges who rule against executive policies? What if a president's administration stops people from peacefully demonstrating or protesting? Or makes it difficult for people to vote? Or interferes with an election or election results? What if the executive acts as a lawmaker and takes over Congress's role? Or keeps the media from criticizing the administration and exposing corruption?

What if the president orders the military to act against US citizens?

Actions like these are not swings of the pendulum from progressive to conservative leadership. They are violations of the law and the Constitution. They are the actions of a dictator. With this kind of rule, the pendulum would stop swinging. Reform would be impossible. Elections would be pointless. And the United States would not be a representative democracy. Americans—progressive, conservative, activist, nonactivist—would lose their republic and their rights. It's a frightening picture.

On January 20, 2025, Republican Donald Trump became president for the second time. He had been elected in 2016 but lost reelection in 2020. He won again in 2024.

Trump immediately directed his aides to shrink many pieces of the federal government. Nearly three hundred thousand government workers lost their jobs without warning or explanation. But civil service laws (supported by progressives) protect federal workers. Those workers are hired for their skills and not because of their political influence. They cannot be fired this way. Not legally.

Trump also demanded that many workers pledge loyalty to him. Yet, by law, these men and women take an oath to follow the US Constitution rather than any one person. They work for the American people, not for a president.

Instead of asking Congress for legislation, he used *executive orders* that don't require approval from Congress. Most presidents have used such orders to manage executive branch operations, not to get around existing laws and the Constitution.

During the first eleven months of his second term, Trump signed 225 executive orders. The previous ten presidents together averaged forty-nine orders per year.[1]

Trump's orders took away money for many federal programs. They demanded the elimination of some federal departments and agencies. But a 1974 law bans presidents from canceling funds that Congress has already approved.

Cuts like these could destroy many of the reforms progressives worked so hard for more than a century ago. They could reverse the achievements made by those who followed the original progressives. They could end government and private programs that today's progressives are working to promote. Progressives are very worried. But they and many others also have even more serious concerns.

President Trump supports banning hundreds of books. He has ordered government agencies, museums, parks, and libraries to remove "divisive" topics from their websites. These topics include important parts of American history such as slavery and Native American history. They include scientific research findings on climate change and health.

The president has approved firing women and people of color in high-ranking military positions. He has ignored the constitutional rights of people being detained and deported. He has deployed national guard troops to cities without approval from governors and mayors.

Will American democracy survive? Will the US Constitution have any meaning?

CHAPTER 21

★★★

Defending Democracy

The United States is in crisis in 2026. Can we look to the women of the Progressive Era to meet today's challenge?

Think of muckraking journalists like Ida B. Wells and Jacob Riis. Or the battle for women's suffrage. Consider the push for laws to make foods and medicines safe. Remember all the letter writing and the marches, protests, and mass meetings that progressive women and others led for so many causes. They were determined and persistent no matter who was in power. Their path to success was slow and difficult. But they never gave up. We can learn from that.

Today's progressive activists are still working for reform. They are also using their skills and experience to fight for democracy. They are not intimidated by power or wealth. And they have formed organizations across the country to encourage other people to join them.

Progressives are not alone in this battle. They stand with all Americans who believe in government by the people. This includes nonpartisan organizations such as the American Civil Liberties Union and the League of Women Voters. It includes the millions of people who attend rallies to support the

Constitution. It includes ordinary citizens who go to their representative's "town hall" meetings to express their anger and fear. It includes political conservatives such as former representatives Liz Cheney and Adam Kinzinger. Both are loyal to the Constitution. They have stood against authoritarian actions since 2020. As a result, both lost their seats in Congress and have received death threats. But they haven't backed down.

The diverse groups and individuals fighting for democracy today share a love of country and loyalty to the Constitution and the rule of law. They disagree with one another on many issues. But their shared democratic principles are enough for this movement. That's all that is required. Those principles—and courage.

Everyone who values democracy can look to earlier courageous people as an example. They can look to the founders who signed the Declaration of Independence, pledging their lives, their fortunes, and their sacred honor. To the men and women who fought for eight bloody years to establish the United States of America. To the thousands of brave Americans who fought with words, work, and weapons to save the United States and end slavery. To the veterans of World War II who gave everything to defeat fascism. To the civil rights activists of the 1960s who faced arrest and abuse over and over but did not back down.

Everyone who values democracy can also look to the women reformers of the Progressive Era. They were determined, persistent, and persuasive. They rejected violence and refused to be intimidated or afraid of arrest. They worked to build community and to find a path toward a more perfect union. No matter how often they met with defeat, or what weaknesses they had, they kept working, kept moving. They followed Sarah Platt Decker's motto, "Never frown, never sigh, keep step." That's still good advice for those who have joined today's struggle.

But perhaps there's another message from those women too. A message for anyone who sees the danger the United States faces today but hasn't acted yet. A message for anyone who knows that democracy always needs defenders. Anyone who hopes that someone, somewhere, will protect and preserve democracy, but doesn't think that *they* are that someone. Listen to Lillian Wald.

"In times of need . . . act."

★★★

Acknowledgments

The Progressive Era is a vast topic with hundreds of potential subtopics. Narrowing it down and zeroing in on representative reformers presented challenges. In the process, I developed an ever-greater appreciation for the academics whose work I rely on in writing for young readers. They spend time, effort, and expertise delving into the lives of people whose names are relatively unknown but whose legacies touch us all. They make books like mine possible.

My thanks to New York's Tenement Museum's staff for their care in keeping the stories of the Lower East Side and its people alive. Thanks also to librarians everywhere who are always ready to assist in finding information, pictures, and so much more, especially at the Willard Public Library in Evansville, Indiana, and the Kiplinger Research Library at the DC History Center in Washington, DC.

Thank you to the extraordinary team at Atheneum Books for Young Readers for making my work better through their creativity, thoughtful suggestions, talent, skill, and patience, and to my editor Julia McCarthy for seeing this through. A big thanks to my agent, Susan Hawk at Upstart Crow, whose constant good cheer, humor, and encouragement are a joy. And to Dr. Michael O'Malley, professor of history at George Mason University, for his thoughtful reading of the manuscript and for his suggestions. I also want to thank Jon Carl, social studies teacher at at F.J. Reitz High School in Evansville, Indiana, and the students who produced a wonderful video on Albion Bacon.

I could not complete any book without relying on family and friends who willingly listen to me drone on, worry aloud, and whine now and then. A special thanks to Milde Waterfall, who jumped in on a moment's notice to read and critique and save me from myself. Also to my nephew Matthew O'Connell, who took pictures of Marne Castle in Denver. And always, my appreciation for my husband, Paul, whose support cannot be measured.

★★★

Selected Bibliography

"1890 Census Bulletins—Manufacturing and Industry." United States Census Bureau, January 1, 1890. https://www.census.gov/library/publications/1890/dec/bulletins/manufacturing-and-industry.html.

"(1898) Mary Church Terrell, 'The Progress of Colored Women.'" BlackPast, November 21, 2011. https://www.blackpast.org/african-american-history/1904-mary-church-terrell-progress-colored-women/.

Allen, Frederick Lewis. *The Big Change: America Transforms Itself, 1900–1950.* Harper & Bros., 1952.

"Average Annual Population of NYC Neighborhoods, 2016–2020." New York State Department of Health, February 2023. https://censusreporter.org/profiles/79500US3604103-nyc-manhattan-community-district-3-lower-east-side-chinatown-puma-ny/.

Bacon, Albion Fellows. *Beauty for Ashes.* Dodd, Mead, 1914; reprint Legare Street Press, 2022.

Barr, Jason, and Teddy Ort. "Population Density Across the City: The Case of 1900 Manhattan." Newark Working Paper #WP2014-005, Rutgers University, March 2014. https://sasn.rutgers.edu/sites/default/files/2024-02/ManhattanDensityApril2014.pdf.

Barrows, Robert G. *Albion Fellows Bacon: Indiana's Municipal Housekeeper.* Indiana University Press, 2000.

Berdy, Judith. "They Lived in a Short-Lived World of Glitz and Glamour." Roosevelt Island Historical Society, "From the Archive" series, June 26, 2021. https://rihs.us/2021/06/26/weekend-june-26-27-2021-they-lived-in-a-short-lived-world-of-glitz-and-glamour/.

"Biography." In "Papers of Leonora O'Reilly, 1861–1928." Schlesinger Library, Radcliffe Institute. https://hollisarchives.lib.harvard.edu/repositories/8/resources/11914.

Cardoza-Oquendo, Juan. "Lugenia Burns Hope." *New Georgia Encyclopedia.* https://www.georgiaencyclopedia.org/articles/history-archaeology/lugenia-burns-hope-1871-1947/.

Chambers, John Whiteclay, II. *The Tyranny of Change: America in the Progressive Era, 1890–1920.* St. Martin's Press, 1992; reprint Rutgers University Press, 2006.

Chirhart, Ann Short. "Lugenia Burns Hope (1871–1947): Fulfilling a Sacred Purpose." In *Georgia Women: Their Lives and Times,* vol. 2, Ann Short Chirhart and Kathleen Ann Clark, eds. University of Georgia Press, 2014, 13–39.

Clayton, Obie, and June Gary Hopps. "Hope Arrives for Atlanta: Lugenia Burns Hope and the Role of Women in the Development of the Atlanta University School of Social Work." *Phylon* 57, no. 2 (Winter 2020): 41–55.

Collens, Jacklyn. "Cultivating Solidarity: Leonora O'Reilly, Working-Class Women, and Middle-Class Allies in the American Woman Suffrage Movement." Master's thesis, Sarah Lawrence College, 2016.

Coss, Clare, ed. *Lillian D. Wald: Progressive Activist.* Feminist Press at the City University of New York, 1989.

Daniels, Doris Groshen. *Always a Sister: The Feminism of Lillian D. Wald.* Feminist Press at the City University of New York, 1989.

Decker, Sarah Platt. "Some Common Questions Answered." New York City National American Woman Suffrage Association. Library of Congress, 1913. https://www.loc.gov/resource/rbpe.13201000/?st=gallery.

Decker, Sarah S. Platt. "The Meaning of the Women's Club Movement." In *American Feminism: Key Source Documents, 1848–1920.* Volume IV: *Women's Clubs and Settlements*, Katherine Joslin, ed. Routledge, 2002. Originally published in *The Annuals of the American Academy of Political and Social Science*, no. 513, 1906.

Duncan, Elizabeth. "Sarah Platt Decker." *Colorado Encyclopedia.* https://coloradoencyclopedia.org/article/sarah-platt-decker.

"Early Chicago: The 1893 World's Fair." *DuSable to Obama: Chicago's Black Metropolis.* WTTW. https://interactive.wttw.com/dusable-to-obama/1893-worlds-fair.

Fee, Elizabeth, and Liping Bu. "The Origins of Public Health Nursing:

The Henry Street Visiting Nurse Service." *American Journal of Public Health* (July 2010): 1206–1207. https://doi.org/10.2105/AJPH.2009.186049.

Filiaci, Anne M. *Lillian Wald—Public Health Progressive.* https://www.lillianwald.com.

Folsom, Burton W. "John D. Rockefeller and the Oil Industry." Foundation for Economic Education, October 1, 1988. https://fee.org/articles/john-d-rockefeller-and-the-oil-industry/.

"The Gilded Age." Andrew Carnegie: The Richest Man in the World. *American Experience.* PBS. https://www.pbs.org/wgbh/americanexperience/features/carnegie-gilded/.

Gould, Lewis L. *America in the Progressive Era, 1890–1914.* Pearson Educational Limited, 2001.

Hertog, Susan. "Partners Against Misery: A Loyal Funder and a Visionary Took on Tenement Squalor, and Won." *Philanthropy Roundtable* (Fall 2016). https://www.philanthropyroundtable.org/magazine/fall-2016-partners-against-misery/.

Hillstrom, Kevin. *The Progressive Era.* Lucent Books, 2008.

Holzer, Harry J. "Is Another Progressive Era Coming? Thoughts on 'The Upswing' by Putnam and Garrett." Brookings, November 10, 2020. https://www.brookings.edu/articles/is-another-progressive-era-coming/.

"Jacob Riis: Revealing 'How the Other Half Lives.'" Library of Congress Exhibitions. https://www.loc.gov/exhibits/jacob-riis/riis-and-reform.html.

Kaplan, Paul M. *Lillian Wald: America's Great Social and Healthcare Reformer.* Pelican Publishing Company, 2018.

Kuhn, Clifford, and Gregory Mixon. "Atlanta Race Massacre of 1906." *New Georgia Encyclopedia*, September 23, 2005. https://www.georgiaencyclopedia.org/articles/history-archaeology/atlanta-race-massacre-of-1906/.

"Labor Wars in the U.S." The Mine Wars: Timeline. *American Experience.* PBS, September 3, 2019. https://www.pbs.org/wgbh/americanexperience/features/theminewars-labor-wars-us/.

Lasch-Quinn, Elisabeth. *Black Neighbors: Race and the Limits of Reform in the American Settlement House Movement, 1890–1945.* University of North Carolina Press, 1993.

"Laura Lyon White." National Park Service. https://www.nps.gov/people/laura-lyon-white.htm.

"Leonora O'Reilly." Archives of Women's Political Communication, Iowa State University. https://awpc.cattcenter.iastate.edu/directory/leonora-oreilly/.

Lewis, Alfred Allan. *Ladies and Not-So-Gentle Women.* Penguin Books, 2001.

"Lillian Wald." *Women of Valor.* Jewish Women's Archive. https://jwa.org/womenofvalor/wald.

"The Lower East Side." *Immigration and Relocation in U.S. History.* Library of Congress. https://www.loc.gov/classroom-materials/immigration/polish-russian/the-lower-east-side/.

"Lower East Side." Tenement Museum. https://www.tenement.org/explore/lower-east-side/.

Lux, Michael. *The Progressive Revolution: How the Best in America Came to Be.* Wiley, 2009.

Mattina, Anne F. "'Rights as Well as Duties': The Rhetoric of Leonora O'Reilly." *Communication Quarterly* 42, no. 2 (Spring 1994): 196–205. https://www.researchgate.net/publication/254254190_Rights_as_Well_as_Duties_The_Rhetoric_of_Leonora_O%27Reilly.

McGerr, Michael. *A Fierce Discontent: The Rise and Fall of the Progressive Movement in America.* Oxford University Press, 2005.

Mintz, Steven. "Statistics: Education in America, 1860–1950." History Resources. Gilder Lehrman Institute of American History. https://www.gilderlehrman.org/history-resources/teacher-resources/statistics-education-america-1860-1950.

Mitchell, Robert. "Andrew Carnegie Built 1,700 Public Libraries. But Some Towns Refused the Steel Baron's Money." *Washington Post,* April 9, 2018. https://www.washingtonpost.com/news/retropolis/wp/2018/04/09/andrew-carnegie-built-1700-public-libraries-but-some-towns-refused-the-steel-barons-money/.

Moody-Turner, Shirley, ed. *The Portable Anna Julia Cooper.* Penguin Books, 2022.

O'Reilly, Leonora. "Statement to the Joint Committee of the Committee on Woman Suffrage and the Committee on the Judiciary, U.S. Senate - March 13, 1912," Iowa State University Archives of Women's Political Communication, https://awpc.cattcenter.iastateedu/2019/07/25/statement-to-the-joint-committee-of-the-committee-on-woman-suffrage-and-the-committee-on-the-judiciary-u-s-senate-march-13-1912/.

Parker, Alison M. *Unceasing Militant: The Life of Mary Church Terrell.* University of North Carolina Press, 2020.

"Progress in Public Health." *The Indiana Historian*, March 1998, p. 3. https://www.in.gov/history/files/publichealth.pdf#:~:text=In%20the%20seventeenth%2C%20eigh%2D%20teenth%2C%20and%20nineteenth,fever%2C%20and%20cholera%20also%20killed%20many%20people.

Putnam, Robert D. *The Upswing: How America Came Together a Century Ago and How We Can Do It Again.* Simon & Schuster, 2020.

Quigley, Joan. *Just Another Southern Town: Mary Church Terrell and the Struggle for Racial Justice in the Nation's Capital.* Oxford University Press, 2016.

Report of the Henry Street Settlement, 1893–1913. Published by the Henry Street Settlement on Its Twentieth Anniversary, January 31, 1913. https://digirepo.nlm.nih.gov/ext/dw/101513893X1/PDF/101513893X1.pdf.

Richardson, Heather Cox. *Democracy Awakening: Notes on the State of America.* Viking, 2023.

Rockefeller, John D. *Random Reminiscences of Men and Events.* Originally published by Doubleday, Page & Co., 1909. https://www.goodreads.com/work/quotes/1255020-random-reminiscences-of-men-and-events.

Rouse, Jacqueline Anne. "The Legacy of Community Organizing: Lugenia Burns Hope and the Neighborhood Union." *Journal of Negro History* 69, nos. 3–4 (Summer–Fall 1984). https://doi.org/10.2307/2717617.

Rouse, Jacqueline Anne. *Lugenia Burns Hope: Black Southern Reformer.* University of Georgia Press, 1989.

Smith, Helena Huntington. "Rampant But Respectable." *The New Yorker*, December 6, 1929. https://www.newyorker.com/magazine/1929/12/14/rampant-but-respectable.

Smith, Jessica. "Henry Street Settlement." *History of Health in New York*, May 20, 2019. https://blogs.baruch.cuny.edu/histmed3450/.

Snyder-Grenier, Ellen M. *The House on Henry Street: The Enduring Life of a Lower East Side Settlement.* Washington Mews Books, 2020.

Stimson, Julia C. *Finding Themselves: The Letters of an American Army Chief Nurse in a British Hospital in France.* Macmillan, 1918. https://www.gutenberg.org/files/58684/58684-h/58684-h.htm.

Tocqueville, Alexis de. *Democracy in America: Volume 2.* Vintage Books, 1945.

Trachenberg, Leo. "Philanthropy That Worked." *City Journal*

(Winter 1998). https://www.city-journal.org/article/philanthropy-that-worked.

Vapnek, Lara. *Breadwinners: Working Women and Economic Independence, 1865–1920.* University of Illinois Press, 2009.

"Volunteers in Action: GFWC Colorado with Mesa Verde National Park." General Federation of Women's Clubs, October 9, 2019. https://www.gfwc.org/volunteers-in-action-gfwc-colorado-with-mesa-verde-national-park/.

Wald, Lillian D. *The House on Henry Street.* Abraham Phillips, illus. Henry Holt & Co., 1915. Released by Project Gutenberg, July 17, 2022. https://www.gutenberg.org/cache/epub/68546/pg68546-images.html.

Waldman, Louis. *Labor Lawyer.* E. P. Dutton, 1944.

Ware, Susan. "Overlooked No More: Leonora O'Reilly, Suffragist Who Fought for Working Women." *New York Times*, August 21, 2020. https://www.nytimes.com/2020/08/21/obituaries/leonora-oreilly-overlooked.html.

Watson, Paula D. "Founding Mothers: The Contribution of Women's Organizations to Public Library Development in the United States." *The Library Quarterly (Chicago)* 64, no. 3 (1994): 233–69. https://doi.org/10.1086/602699.

"What Is a Public Health Nurse?" Nursing, History, and Health Care. Penn Nursing, University of Pennsylvania. https://www.nursing.upenn.edu/nhhc/home-care/what-is-a-public-health-nurse/.

"Women's Suffrage Movement." *Colorado Encyclopedia.* https://coloradoencyclopedia.org/article/womens-suffrage-movement#Advantages-and-Victory.

"World's Columbian Exposition." *Encyclopedia of Chicago.* http://www.encyclopedia.chicagohistory.org/pages/1386.html.

★★★

Endnotes

Chapter 1: The Very Wealthy

1. Anne de Courcy, "Mrs Astor Invites," *Beyond: The St. Regis Magazine*, https://magazine.stregis.com/mrs-astor-invites-2/.
2. Berdy, "They Lived in a Short-Lived World."
3. Patrick J. Kiger, "How Robber Barons Flaunted Their Money During the Gilded Age," History, January 24, 2022, https://www.history.com/news/robber-barons-gilded-age-wealth?cmpid=email-hist-inside-history-2022-0124-0124.
4. Ibid.
5. "The Gilded Age," https://www.pbs.org/wgbh/americanexperience/features/carnegie-gilded/.
6. Heather Angel, "10 Fast Facts About Biltmore: Estate History," Biltmore, September 18, 2018, https://www.biltmore.com/blog/10-fast-facts-about-biltmore/.
7. Hillstrom, 18.
8. McGerr, 7.
9. "J. P. Morgan: American Financier," *Britannica Money*, June 21, 2025, https://www.britannica.com/money/J-P-Morgan.
10. Rockefeller, *Random Reminiscences*.

Chapter 2: The Working Poor

1. Barr and Ort, 2, 4.
2. "Average Annual Population of NYC Neighborhoods, 2016–2020," https://censusreporter.org/profiles/79500US3604103-nyc-manhattan-community-district-3-lower-east-side-chinatown-puma-ny/.

3. "Jacob Riis," https://www.loc.gov/exhibits/jacob-riis/riis-and-reform.html.
4. "City of Workers, City of Struggle Lesson: 'We Are One,'" Museum of the City of New York, https://www.mcny.org/lesson-plans/city-workers-city-struggle-lesson-we-are-one.
5. "The Steel Business," Andrew Carnegie: The Richest Man in the World, *American Masters*, PBS, https://www.pbs.org/wgbh/americanexperience/features/carnegie-steel-business/.
6. Chambers, 2, 87.
7. Ibid., 67.
8. Ana Hernández Kent, "The State of U.S. Household Wealth," Federal Reserve Bank of St. Louis, https://www.stlouisfed.org/institute-for-economic-equity/the-state-of-us-wealth-inequality.
9. Noah Kirsch, "The 3 Richest Americans Hold More Wealth Than Bottom 50% of the Country, Study Finds," *Forbes*, November 9, 2017, https://www.forbes.com/sites/noahkirsch/2017/11/09/the-3-richest-americans-hold-more-wealth-than-bottom-50-of-country-study-finds/?sh=1dd2bcd93cf8.
10. "The Steel Business."
11. Josh Bivens and Jori Kandra, "CEO Pay Has Skyrocketed 1,460% Since 1978," Economic Policy Institute, October 4, 2022, https://www.epi.org/publication/ceo-pay-in-2021/.

Chapter 3: From the Middle

1. Anne M. Filiaci, "Childhood," *Lillian Wald—Public Health Progressive*," https://www.lillianwald.com/?page_id=6.
2. McGerr, 43; and Rakesh Kochhar and Stella Sechopoulos, "How the American Middle Class Has Changed in the Past Five Decades," Pew Research Center, April 20, 2022, https://www.pewresearch.org/short-reads/2022/04/20/how-the-american-middle-class-has-changed-in-the-past-five-decades/.
3. Trachenberg, "Philanthropy That Worked."
4. Mintz, "Statistics."
5. "The Gilded Age."

Chapter 4: Intersections

1. Kaplan, 21.
2. Wald, 5.
3. Ibid., 5–6.
4. Ibid., 2.

5. Thomas D. Snyder, ed. *120 Years of American Education: A Statistical Portrait*, National Center for Education Statistics, January 1993, https://nces.ed.gov/pubs93/93442.pdf.
6. Kaplan, 23.
7. Hertog, "Partners Against Misery."
8. Ibid.
9. Kaplan, 49.
10. Smith, "Rampant But Respectable."
11. Kaplan, 50.
12. McGerr, 36.
13. "Our History," The Rockefeller Foundation, https://www.rockefellerfoundation.org/about-us/our-history/.
14. "Andrew Carnegie Quotes," AZ Quotes, https://www.azquotes.com/quote/353367.
15. "Bloomberg Millionaires Index," Bloomberg, accessed September 19, 2025, https://www.bloomberg.com/billionaires/.
16. Devin Sean Martin, "The 2023 Forbes 400: The 20 Richest People in America," *Forbes*, October 3, 2023, https://www.forbes.com/sites/devinseanmartin/2023/10/03/the-2023-forbes-400-the-20-richest-people-in-america/?sh=1041c1f3571f.

Chapter 5: The House on Henry Street

1. Wald, 83–85.
2. Wald, 89.
3. Kaplan, 30.
4. Snyder-Grenier, 54.
5. Wald, 53.
6. Ibid., 18.
7. Ibid., 18–19.
8. Ibid., 165.
9. Snyder-Grenier, 55.
10. Ibid., 60.
11. Snyder-Grenier, 61–62.
12. Ibid., 62.
13. Wald, 46.
14. Fee and Bu, "The Origins of Public Health Nursing."
15. "Our History," VNS Health, https://www.vnshealth.org/about/our-history/.
16. "About," Henry Street Settlement, https://www.henrystreet.org/about/.

Chapter 6: The Homes of Indiana

1. Barrows, 24.
2. Bacon, 22.
3. Ibid., 7–8.
4. Ibid., 24.
5. Ibid., 25.
6. "Progress in Public Health," 3.
7. Bacon, 27.
8. Ibid., 29.
9. Ibid., 38.
10. Ibid., 173.
11. Ibid., 96.

Chapter 7: Municipal Housekeeping

1. Bacon, 107–108.
2. Ibid., 163.
3. Ibid., 164.
4. Ibid., 165.
5. Ibid., 169.
6. Ibid., 170.
7. Ibid.

Chapter 8: A Widening Sphere

1. Barrows, 94.
2. Bacon, 171.
3. Ibid., 173.
4. Ibid., 176.
5. Ibid., 181.
6. Barrows, 70.
7. Bacon, 185–186.
8. Ibid., 188.
9. Ibid., 189.
10. Ibid., 189–193.
11. Barrows, 57–59.
12. Ibid., 64.
13. Ibid., 66.
14. "Democrats Believe They Worked Well." *Fort Wayne News and Sentinel*, March 7, 1911, https://www.newspapers.com/image/29298197/?terms=bacon&match=1.

15. Barrows, 76.
16. Ibid., 85.
17. Ibid., 58.
18. Ibid., 80.

Chapter 9: Stark Reality

1. Rouse, *Lugenia Burns Hope*, 16–17.
2. United States Census Bureau, https://daily.jstor.org/the-worlds-fair-that-ignored-more-than-half-the-world/.
3. "Fair or Not: Workers at the 1893 World's Columbian Exposition," Chicago History Museum, https://condor.depaul.edu/tps/resources/chicago/chm/Fair_or_not_teachers.pdf.
4. "Timeline." World's Fair Chicago, 1893, https://worldsfairchicago1893.com/home/fair/timeline/.
5. Rouse, *Lugenia Burns Hope*, 21, 24.
6. Ibid., 29.
7. Clayton and Hopps, 42.
8. Mary Jo Deegan, "W.E.B. Du Bois and the Women of Hull-House, 1895–1899," *The American Sociologist* 19, no. 4 (1988): 301–11. http://www.jstor.org/stable/27698433.
9. Rouse, *Lugenia Burns Hope*, 28–29.

Chapter 10: Community Organizing

1. Rouse, *Lugenia Burns Hope*, 42.
2. Ibid., 43.
3. Kuhn and Mixon. "Atlanta Race Massacre of 1906."
4. Chirhart, 23.
5. Rouse, *Lugenia Burns Hope*, 66.
6. Lasch-Quinn, 113.
7. Chirhart, 27.
8. Rouse, "The Legacy of Community Organizing," 118.
9. Rouse, *Lugenia Burns Hope*, 71.
10. Ibid., 79.

Chapter 11: "I Know Whereof I Speak"

1. Vapnek, 140.
2. Leonora O'Reilly, "Statement to the Joint Committee of the Committee on Woman Suffrage and the Committee on the Judiciary, U.S. Senate - March 13, 1912," Iowa State University Archives

of Women's Political Communication, https://awpc.cattcenter.iastate.edu/2019/07/25/statement-to-the-joint-committee-of-the-committee-on-woman-suffrage-and-the-committee-on-the-judiciary-u-s-senate-march-13-1912/.
3. Vapnek, 69.
4. Ibid., 139.
5. Ibid., 70.
6. Ibid., 72.
7. Ibid., 101.
8. Ibid., 74.
9. Ibid., 75.
10. Ibid., 74–76.
11. Anne M. Filiaci, "Leonora O'Reilly and the Model Shirtwaist Shop at the Henry Street Settlement," *Lillian Wald—Public Health Progressive*, https://www.lillianwald.com/?page_id=482.

Chapter 12: Agitating

1. Filiaci, "Leonora O'Reilly and the Model Shirtwaist Shop."
2. Ibid.
3. Vapnek, 151.
4. Mattina, 196.
5. Ibid.
6. Vapnek, 151.
7. Mattina, 196.
8. Vapnek, 129–130.
9. Mattina, 200.
10. Ibid., 202.
11. Waldman, 32–33.
12. Ware, "Overlooked No More."
13. O'Reilly, "Statement to the Joint Committee."
14. "Stories from the Past: Luisa Capetillo," Historical Legacies, National Museum of the American Latino, https://latino.si.edu/exhibitions/presente/historical-legacies.
15. CEPR, "Union Membership and Income Inequality," Center for Economic and Policy Research, September 9, 2015, https://www.cepr.net/union-membership-and-income-inequality/.
16. "Union Members—2024," News Release, Bureau of Labor Statistics, U.S. Department of Labor, January 28, 2025, https://www.bls.gov/news.release/pdf/union2.pdf.

17. Michael Sainato, "'They Are Breaking the Law': Inside Amazon's Bid to Stall a Union Drive," *The Guardian*, April 3, 2024, https://www.theguardian.com/technology/2024/apr/03/amazon-union-warehouse-california.
18. "Fact Sheet: Treasury Department Releases First-of-Its-Kind Report on Benefits of Unions to the U.S. Economy," Press Releases, U.S. Department of the Treasury, August 28, 2023, https://home.treasury.gov/news/press-releases/jy1706.
19. https://www.afscme.org/blog/gallup-poll-americans-support-for-unions-remains-strong-near-all-time-highs.

Chapter 13: "Never Frown, Never Sigh"

1. "About Us," Sarah Platt Decker Chapter, NSDAR, 2025, https://sarahplattdecker.coloradodar.org/about-us/.
2. "Women's Suffrage Movement." *Colorado Encyclopedia*, https://coloradoencyclopedia.org/article/womens-suffrage-movement#Advantages-and-Victory.
3. "Sarah Platt Decker," *Colorado Encyclopedia*, https://coloradoencyclopedia.org/article/sarah-platt-decker.

Chapter 14: "Keep Step"

1. Tocqueville, 199.
2. "Colonel Platt Dead," *Colorado Transcript*, August, 15, 1894, https://www.coloradohistoricnewspapers.org/?a=d&d=CTR18940815.2.17&e=-------en-20--1--img-txIN%7ctxCO%7ctxTA--------0------.
3. "Sarah Platt Decker," *Colorado Encyclopedia*.
4. "Sarah Platt Decker," Person Record, Women's History and Resource Center, https://gfwc.catalogaccess.com/people/1013.
5. Rheta Childe Dorr, "From Culture Clubs to Social Service," chap. 2 in *What Eight Million Women Want*, 1910, p. 41, released by Project Gutenberg, May 1, 2004, https://www.gutenberg.org/cache/epub/12226/pg12226-images.html#Page_41.
6. Watson, 249.
7. "The Bennett Square Building (which as of 2015 is called the Georgian Center) on Main Street in Wheeling, West Virginia, Library of Congress, https://www.loc.gov/item/2015632083/.
8. Mitchell, "Andrew Carnegie Built 1,700 Public Libraries."
9. Watson, 235–237; and Anne Firor Scott, "Women and Libraries," *The*

Journal of Library History (1974–1987) 21, no. 2 (1986): 400–405, http://www.jstor.org/stable/25541703.

Chapter 15: For Better and Worse

1. Upton Sinclair, *The Jungle*, Doubleday, Page & Co., 1906, 113–117.
2. Ibid.
3. Decker, "The Meaning of the Women's Club Movement."
4. "Women's Clubs: Women and Volunteer Power, 1868–1926 and Beyond," National Women's History Museum, March 17, 2014, https://www.womenshistory.org/articles/womens-clubs.
5. Kristen L. Rouse, "Meat Inspection Act of 1906," *Britannica*, last updated June 23, 2025, https://www.britannica.com/topic/Meat-Inspection-Act.
6. "About GFWC," GFWC Massachusetts, https://www.gfwcma.org/about-gfwc.html.
7. McGerr, 39.
8. "Laura Lyon White," National Park Service.
9. "Sarah S. Platt Decker Leader in Woman's Movement," *The Omaha Sunday Bee*, January 26, 1908, http://www.deckerjourney.com/stories/stories-SarahPlattDecker1908.html.
10. "Sarah Platt Decker," *Colorado Encyclopedia.*
11. "Survey: Proportion of Christians in the U.S. Has Stopped Shrinking," Ethics & Religious Liberty Commission, July 9, 2021, https://erlc.com/policy-content/survey-proportion-of-christians-in-the-u-s-has-stopped-shrinking/.
12. Linda D. Wilson, "Oklahoma Federation of Women's Clubs," *The Encyclopedia of Oklahoma History and Culture*, Oklahoma Historical Society, https://www.okhistory.org/publications/enc/entry?entry=OK046.
13. William Toll, "Club Movement in the United States," *The Shalvi/Hyman Encyclopedia of Jewish Women*, Jewish Women's Archive, https://jwa.org/encyclopedia/article/club-movement-in-united-states.
14. Patricia Dawn Robinson, "From Pedestal to Platform: The American Women's Club Movement, 1800–1920," ProQuest Dissertations & Theses, 1993, https://wrlc-gm.primo.exlibrisgroup.com/discovery/fulldisplay?docid=cdi_proquest_journals_304071697&context=PC&vid=01WRLC_GML:01WRLC_GML&lang=en&search_scope=MyInst_and_CI&adaptor=Primo%20

Central&tab=Everything&query=any,contains,women%27s%20club%20movement&sortby=rank&offset=30.

15. "Who We Are," GFWC, https://www.gfwc.org/who-we-are/.
16. Beth Almeida and Isabela Salas-Betsch, "Fact Sheet: The State of Women in the Labor Market in 2023," Center for American Progress, February 6, 2023, https://www.americanprogress.org/article/fact-sheet-the-state-of-women-in-the-labor-market-in-2023/.

Chapter 16: Other Voices

1. "Mary Church Terrell Speaks at the International Congress of Women, 1904," *The Appeal,* July 16, 1904, p. 2, https://www.newspapers.com/article/the-appeal-mary-church-terrell-speaks-at/46052303/.
2. Parker, 15, 23.
3. Ibid., 24.
4. Ibid., 26.
5. Ibid., 28.
6. Ibid., 39.
7. "Ida B. Wells and the Campaign Against Lynching," Bill of Rights Institute, https://billofrightsinstitute.org/essays/ida-b-wells-and-the-campaign-against-lynching.
8. Ibid.
9. Parker, 51.
10. NAACP, "Platform Adopted by National Negro Committee (1909)," National Constitution Center, https://constitutioncenter.org/the-constitution/historic-document-library/detail/naacp-platform-adopted-by-national-negro-committee-new-york-national-negro-committee-1909.
11. Parker, 49.

Chapter 17: The End of an Era

1. Snyder-Grenier, 63.
2. Stimson, 142.
3. Lewis, 330–334.
4. Ibid., 343.
5. Marjorie Feld, "Sleepless Nights in 1918: Lillian Wald and Henry Street's First Influenza Epidemic," Henry Street Settlement, April 9, 2020, https://www.henrystreet.org/news/latest-news/sleepless-nights-in-1918-lillian-wald-and-henry-streets-first-influenza-epidemic/.

6. "The Pandemic's True Death Toll," *The Economist*, October 25, 2022, https://www.economist.com/graphic-detail/coronavirus-excess-deaths-estimates.
7. "1918 Influenza Pandemic (Spanish Flu)," Cleveland Clinic, last reviewed October 24, 2024, https://my.clevelandclinic.org/health/diseases/21777-spanish-flu.
8. Kareem Crayton, "The Voting Rights Act Explained," Brennan Center for Justice, July 17, 2023, https://www.brennancenter.org/our-work/research-reports/voting-rights-act-explained.
9. Ibid.

Chapter 18: Legacy

1. "Calvin Coolidge Quotations," Calvin Coolidge Presidential Foundation, https://coolidgefoundation.org/quote/quotations-b/.
2. Kat Eschner, "Leaded Gas Was a Known Poison the Day It Was Invented," *Smithsonian Magazine*, December 9, 2016, https://www.smithsonianmag.com/smart-news/leaded-gas-poison-invented-180961368/.
3. Don Vaughan, "Radium Girls: The Women Who Fought for Their Lives in a Killer Workplace," *Britannica*, last updated June 13, 2025, https://www.britannica.com/story/radium-girls-the-women-who-fought-for-their-lives-in-a-killer-workplace.
4. Barrows, 131–132.
5. Ibid.
6. "Prohibition," Digital History, 2021, https://www.digitalhistory.uh.edu/disp_textbook.cfm?smtID=2&psid=3383.
7. Snyder, ed., *120 Years of American Education*.

Chapter 19: New Voices, New Challenges

1. "Our Story," Public Health Solutions, https://www.healthsolutions.org/about-us/our-story/.
2. "Astronaut Nicole Aunapu Mann Answered Questions from Native Students, Indigenous Media in Live Interview from Space Station," Native News Online, October 19, 2022, https://nativenewsonline.net/currents/astronaut-nicole-aunapu-mann-answered-questions-from-native-students-indigenous-media-in-live-interview-from-space-station/.
3. Mariana Brandman, "Alice Wong," National Women's History Museum, 2021, www.womenshistory.org/education-resources/biographies/alice-wong.

4. "Mari Copeny," Iowa State University Archives of Women's Political Communication, https://awpc.cattcenter.iastate.edu/directory/mari-copeny/.
5. Muslims for Progressive Values website, https://www.mpvusa.org/.
6. Robert D. Bullard, "Andrea Vidaurre," "The 100 Most Influential People of 2025," *w*, April 16, 2025, https://time.com/collections/100-most-influential-people-2025/7273791/andrea-vidaurre/.

Chapter 20: A Swing Too Far?

1. "How Many Executive Orders Has Each President Signed?" USAFacts, January 16, 2026, https://usafacts.org/articles/how-many-executive-orders-has-each-president-signed/.

★★★

Photo Credits

Every effort has been made to correctly acknowledge and contact the source and/or copyright holder of each image. Simon & Schuster apologizes for any unintentional errors or omissions, which will be corrected in future printings of this book.

p. 2: Metropolitan Museum of Art, Open Access API, gift of R. Thornton Wilson and Orme Wilson, 1949

p. 4: Library of Congress Prints and Photographs Division, Miscellaneous Items in High Demand

p. 5: Library of Congress Prints and Photographs Division, Gottscho-Schleisner Collection

p. 6: Library of Congress Prints and Photographs Division, Miscellaneous Items in High Demand

p. 8: Library of Congress Prints and Photographs Division, Detroit Publishing Company photograph collection

p. 9: Library of Congress Prints and Photographs Division

p. 10: National Portrait Gallery, Smithsonian Institution; gift of Oswald D. Reich

p. 15: Library of Congress Prints and Photographs Division, Detroit Publishing Company photograph collection

pp. 16–17: Library of Congress Prints and Photographs Division, Panoramic photographs

p. 19: Library of Congress Prints and Photographs Division

p. 20: Library of Congress Prints and Photographs Division, Detroit Publishing Company Collection

p. 21: Library of Congress Prints and Photographs Division, National Photo Company Collection

p. 22 *(both)*: Library of Congress Prints and Photographs Division, National Child Labor Committee collection

p. 23: Library of Congress Prints and Photographs Division, National Child Labor Committee collection

p. 24: Library of Congress Prints and Photographs Division, Postcard filing series (Library of Congress)

p. 25: Library of Congress, Prints & Photographs Division

p. 26: Library of Congress Prints and Photographs Division

p. 30: Pie chart: Irene Metaxatos

p. 35: Brigham Young University

p. 36: Library of Congress Prints and Photographs Division

p. 45: Wikimedia Commons

p. 46: Library of Congress Prints and Photographs Division, Detroit Publishing Company photograph collection

p. 49: *The House on Henry Street* by Lillian D. Wald, https://www.gutenberg.org/cache/epub/68546/pg68546-images.html.

p. 52: Library of Congress Prints and Photographs Division, Bain News Service photograph collection

p. 55: Library of Congress Prints and Photographs Division, Harris & Ewing photograph collection

p. 62: Medical Center Archives of NewYork-Presbyterian/Weill Cornell, New York-Presbyterian/Weill Cornell Medical Center Archives Digital Collection

p. 63: *The House on Henry Stree*t by Lillian D. Wald, https://www.gutenberg.org/cache/epub/68546/pg68546-images.html.

p. 64: Library of Congress Prints and Photographs Division

p. 66: Courtesy of Henry Street Settlement

p. 67: Library of Congress Prints and Photographs Division, New York World-Telegram and the Sun Newspaper Photograph Collection

p. 71: National Portrait Gallery, Smithsonian Institution; gift of the Visiting Nurse Service of New York

p. 73: Visiting Nurse Service of New York

p. 77: Library of Congress Prints and Photographs Division, Bain News Service photograph collection

p. 87: Courtesy of Willard Library, Evansville, Indiana

p. 93: Library of Congress Prints and Photographs Division; Johnston, Frances Benjamin, 1864-1952. Portraits

p. 95: Library of Congress Prints and Photographs Division, Highsmith, Carol M., 1946– Carol M. Highsmith Archive

p. 97: Library of Congress

p. 101: Atlanta University Center Robert W. Woodruff Library, Neighborhood Union Collection

p. 103: Library of Congress Prints and Photographs Division

pp. 104–105: Library of Congress Prints and Photographs Division, Frances Benjamin Johnston Collection

p. 107: Library of Congress, Manuscript Division, The Frederick Douglass Papers collection

p. 108: Atlanta University Center Robert W. Woodruff Library, Neighborhood Union Collection

p. 111: Library of Congress Prints and Photographs Division, Du Bois, W. E. B. (William Edward Burghardt), 1868-1963. Du Bois albums of photographs of African Americans in Georgia exhibited at the Paris Exposition Universelle in 1900

p. 112: Library of Congress Prints and Photographs Division Washington

p. 118: Atlanta University Center Robert W. Woodruff Library, Neighborhood Union Collection

p. 119: Atlanta University Center Robert W. Woodruff Library, Atlanta University Photographs

p. 126: National Portrait Gallery, Smithsonian Institution

p. 129: Metropolitan Museum of Art, Gift of Estate of Valerie Dreyfus, 1957

p. 130: Library of Congress Prints and Photographs Division

p. 142: Library of Congress Prints and Photographs Division

p. 144: Library of Congress Prints and Photographs Division, Bain News Service photograph collection

p. 145: Library of Congress Prints and Photographs Division, Bain News Service photograph collection

p. 147: Franklin D. Roosevelt Library Photographs, National Archives and Records Administration, Graff Collection

p. 148: Franklin D. Roosevelt Library Photographs, National Archives and Records Administration, Graff Collection

p. 149: Schlesinger Library on the History of Women in America, Radcliffe Institute A39-1a-1

p. 157: Library of Congress Prints and Photographs Division

p. 159: Library of Congress Prints and Photographs Division, Popular Graphic Arts

pp. 160–161: Library of Congress Prints and Photographs Division, Detroit Publishing Company Collection

p. 166: Courtesy of Ashley Rene and Clio Admin, "Castle Marne." Clio: Your Guide to History. July 29, 2020. Accessed June 17, 2025. https://theclio.com/entry/107383

p. 173: Library of Congress Prints and Photographs Division, National Photo Company Collection

p. 176: Library of Congress Prints and Photographs Division

p. 178: Library of Congress Prints and Photographs Division

p. 179: National Archives and Records Administration, Sir Henry Wellcome Collection

p. 183: Humboldt County Historical Society

p. 185: iStock.com

p. 186 *(top)*: Library of Congress Prints and Photographs Division, Highsmith, Carol M., 1946– Carol M. Highsmith Archive

p. 186 *(bottom)*: Library of Congress Prints and Photographs, Bain News Service photograph collection

p. 189: Library of Congress Prints and Photographs

p. 190: Jewish Women's Archive

p. 195: Library of Congress Prints and Photographs

p. 197: Kiplinger Research Library, DC History Center

p. 202: Library of Congress Prints and Photographs, Historic American Buildings Survey (Library of Congress)

p. 204: Library of Congress Prints and Photographs

p. 205: Library of Congress Prints and Photographs, George Grantham Bain Collection

p. 206: Library of Congress Prints and Photographs, C.M. Bell Studio

Collection (Library of Congress)

p. 210: Alamy

p. 212: Library of Congress Prints and Photographs, Bain News Service photograph collection

p. 214: Library of Congress Prints and Photographs

p. 216: Library of Congress Prints and Photographs

p. 217: National Archives and Records Administration, American Unofficial Collection of World War I Photographs

p. 224: Library of Congress Prints and Photographs; National Photo Company Collection (Library of Congress)

p. 225: Library of Congress Prints and Photographs

p. 226: Courtesy of Beyond My Ken, Wikipedia

p. 227: Library of Congress Prints and Photographs, National Photo Company Collection (Library of Congress)

p. 229: Marc PoKemper, National Archives and Records Administration

p. 230: Library of Congress Prints and Photographs, New York World-Telegram and the Sun Newspaper Photograph Collection (Library of Congress)

p. 233: Library of Congress Prints and Photographs Division, Harris & Ewing photograph collection

p. 234: National Archives, Harmon Foundation Collection

p. 238: Courtesy of Public Health Solutions

p. 239: NASA/Bill Ingalls

p. 240: © John D. and Catherine T. MacArthur Foundation–used with permission.

p. 241: Pete Souza, Obama White House Archived

p. 242: Ani Zonneveld, Muslims for Progressive Values

p. 243: Andrea Viduarre, People's Collective for Environmental Justice

p. 246: National Archives, America's Founding Documents